DATING DELILAH

PURITY FROM A NEW PERSPECTIVE

JUDAH SMITH

Thanks for reading our daddy's book!

DEDICATION

This book is dedicated to a man I have modeled my life after. I have watched him closely. I have worked to sound like him. I have strived to lead like him. I have practiced to preach like him — even developed my handwriting to copy him.

↳ *Judah & his dad, Dr. Wendell Smith on the 18th hole at Pebble Beach!*

He's my hero.

He is my mom's devoted husband.

He is my Dad.

This book is dedicated to you, Dad.

I love you.

THANKS

Special love
goes to:

My God

My Wife

My Sons

My Mom

My Sister

My Pastor, Jude
Fouquier

My Team, the
Generation
Church staff

Melissa Wirasnik

Sean & Casey
Sperte

Andy & Kacee
Jensen

Michael Vossler

THE CITY CHURCH™

Originally published by The City Church, 2008
9051 132nd Ave NE, Kirkland, WA 98033, USA
425-803-3233 | thecity.org

Produced by Chelsea Smith, Gini Smith & Casey Sperte

Cover design & art direction by Sean Sperte

Design & layout by Michelle DeMonnin, DeMonnin's Art Studio, Inc.

Edited by Melissa Wirasnik & Cathy Maddox

TABLE OF CONTENTS

FOREWORD SHAUN ALEXANDER

When I was younger I was told that Satan's three greatest generals where Gold, Glory, and Girls. General Gold represented the love of money. He'd say, "with money all your desires will be met." General Glory represented pride: "fame and power is all you need in life." General Girls (Lust) represented the lust of the flesh. She'd smoothly whisper, "I can satisfy you, I will make you happy forever."

All three are incredible liars, taught by their father Satan (the King of Liars). Their job is to get the world hooked on them instead of God's good and perfect will for their life. The Bible says in **MATTHEW 6:24**, "No one can serve two masters, either he will hate the one and love the other, or he will be devoted to one and despise the other. You can't serve both God and money." These three generals of Satan know the Bible well, just like their daddy does, and they have been manipulating scriptures to get society to miss everything that God wants them to have: real love and real life!

It's crazy to think that our society will mention that money isn't everything. Society will say things like "love doesn't cost a thing." This fires up General Gold to work harder to get you to chase after money. Starting with grade school you're told to go to school to get the good grades; you get the good grades to get in college. Then you go to college to get the great job; you get the great job to get the great pay; leave that job for a better paying job, and the cycle after General Gold is on.

Society will also say, "watch what you say, nobody likes an arrogant know it all" or, as it says in **PROVERBS 16:18**, "Pride comes before destruction, a haughty spirit before the fall." In so many ways society says to each other: don't be arrogant or look down on others. Yet at the same time we'll admire some of the most prideful people or actions that happen around us. Then we crave acceptance from those people or by doing those things. The next step is aligning ourselves to those people or those situations and then the chase for General Glory is in motion.

As evil and detracting as General Gold and General Glory are, there is no general more vicious than the General of Lust. She is smooth. When you first meet her it seems unintentional, but like I said, she is smooth. You were in her sight long before you even saw her. She is very intentional. She studies you from the beginning, finding ways to get your attention and make it look like you found her when actually the whole time this was a part of her plan. Her next

step is to get you focused on you. That could be by letting you notice the piece of your life that she can fill or it could be in giving you easy access to fulfilling lustful desires you have in your heart. Both are real things. Let's take the story in **PROVERBS 7**:

"I saw among the simple, I noticed among the young men, a youth who lacked judgment."
— **PROVERBS 7:7 & 8**

He was going down the street near her corner, walking near her house.

"So I came out to meet you; I looked for you and have found you!" — **PROVERBS 7:15**

He was by himself and she said, "hey I can fill that void."

"I have perfumed my bed with myrrh, aloes, and cinnamon. Come, let's drink deep of love till morning; lets enjoy ourselves with love!"
— **PROVERBS 7:17 & 18**

This is the easy access to fulfill lustful desires.

This General of Lust is so powerful because most of the time we don't fight against this General; we fight against the person. We'll say to our struggling brother/sister, "don't do that", or "you shouldn't be living like this", or "ya'll messed up again"; allowing this smooth, subtle General of Lust to break you down from the inside out.

Often General Glory works with Her. General Glory swoops in to whisper to you, "you're a hypocrite. How're you going to tell someone about her when you have lost to her too?" So you fall for the lie. You even get to the point where you don't tell your real, full testimony when asked. You share a false testimony, giving General Pride enough power to protect the General of Lust. At the end the General of Lust is never dealt with.

So what happens? It tells us in **PROVERBS 7:21-23**:

"With persuasive words she led him astray; she seduced him with her smooth talk. All at once he followed her like an ox going to slaughter, like a deer stepping into a noose til an arrow pierces his liver, like a bird darting into a snare, little knowing it will cost him his life."

So what happens to you? You lose the perfect will of God. You have wars that you never intended to fight. You gain scars you never were supposed to have. The Bible is clear when it says in **1 CORINTHIANS 6:18** "flee sexual immorality. All other sins a man commits are outside the body, but he who sins sexually sins against his own body." Sexual sin changes how you think, act, and look at the world and yourself.

We need a solution, and Jesus is always the way. **HOSEA 4:6** says, "My people perish from a lack of knowledge." Let's live with God's knowledge towards dating, towards relationships, and towards sex.

Judah Smith is one of the greatest pastors in the world. He is anointed by God to teach the youth of the world how to boldly confess Jesus as King and live like a servant of God. Dating Delilah will give you knowledge and truth that will set you free from misunderstandings in relationships that came from family traditions or society's ways of thinking. Let this book help mold you into the child of God you need to be. Grow with Jesus. Walk as he walked and live as he lived. Stay away from the General of Lust. She has one goal and it's similar to her father's — it is to steal, to kill, and to destroy.

Or, as it says at the end of **PROVERBS 7**:

"Now then, my sons, listen to me; pay attention to what I say. Do not let your heart turn to her ways or stray into her paths. Many are the victims she has brought down; her slain are a mighty throng. Her house is a highway to the grave, leading down to the chambers of death."

Do the Extraordinary. Live for Purity

—Shaun Alexander

Chapter 1
THE BEAUTIFUL AFFLICTION

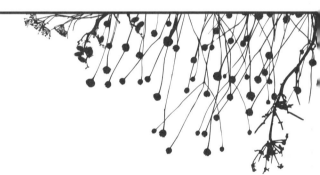

Sex is beautiful. God made it beautiful. God is into sex. In the beginning God made man and woman naked and unashamed. He created you with a sex drive and His original intention was for people to enjoy sex. Although God's design for sex has been compromised, He is not intimidated by the perversion of what was intended to be beautiful. God is not in heaven wringing His hands and wondering, "What am I going to do with sex?" I believe that God wants to restore the beauty of sexuality by revealing His original plan and the context in which it is meant to be enjoyed.

I'm not afraid to talk about sex. **We have to talk about sex because what was meant to be beautiful has become an affliction for many people.** Remember the movie "A Bug's Life?" In the beginning of the movie there is a scene set on the porch of an old mobile home where two flies are buzzing around. One fly is mesmerized by a captivating light which he doesn't realize is coming from a bug zapper. He flies straight at the light, proclaiming that "it's so beautiful." Even though this fly's friend begs him not to look at the light, he can't resist the temptation to get a closer look and his life ends with a large zap! It's a beautiful affliction.

Some, like the mesmerized fly, are captivated by lust and sex, thinking it will satisfy in any context. Sex is only beautiful in the right context at the right time. Everything is beautiful in its time, but something taken out of that time and context can quickly become an affliction. If misused, what God intended for beauty and love can actually destroy your

destiny. It is critical that we look to the Bible to find out what God's Word says about sexual relationships.

I had no idea that the first day of 1999 would change my life. It was the day of my first date and, at 20 years old, I was ready. After seeking the approval of my father, her father, and all of my pastors, I took my long-time friend Chelsea to a local restaurant perched at the bottom of an awe inspiring waterfall. Wow! She looked good! After eating dinner, which I barely touched, we took a walk up to the viewing bridge at Multnomah Falls. It was there that I planned to ask the big question.

↳ *Judah & Chelsea on their first date at Multnomah Falls.*

Now ladies, I know you're thinking, "Oh my gosh, he asked her to marry him on the first date, how romantic," but slow down. I had memorized a speech before the date, but as we stood at that romantic place, my mind went blank I blurted out, "uh... Pastor Jude (my youth pastor) said I could hold your hand!" The look on Chelsea's face said it all. She stood there stunned, wondering whether I was asking or telling her to

Judah & Chelsea in 2007, married eight years →

hold my hand. I didn't turn out to be the smooth operator I envisioned myself to be but, now married, we laugh when we rehearse the memory. By the way, Chelsea did hold my hand and it was like experiencing the Fourth of July in January! My story isn't smooth but it is pure. Chelsea and I have no regrets or shame from our season of dating, just the way God intended.

When the right time and right person come along, God wants your romantic relationship to be a beautiful, exhilarating adventure — an adventure marked by purity. I'm on a mission sent by God to restore beauty back to your sexuality. You can live pure.

A PROPHETIC PICTURE

In LUKE 7:11-17 we see a prophetic picture of this generation. In this chapter, Jesus enters a city called Nain where He comes upon a funeral procession for a young man being carried out to burial. As the story goes, Jesus is moved by the tears of the boy's mother and

interrupts the funeral by calling the young man to life! This story, of the first person Jesus raises from the dead, paints a symbolic picture of the current state of our generation. The dead young man being carried from the city is typical of today's young person — dead in sin, surrendered to compromise, and yielded to cultural trends.

It is important to point out that the young man in the story is from Nain — a word which means "beauty" and "afflicted". For this particular boy and his mother, Nain was a place of affliction. Similarly, sexuality has become a place of torment rather than beauty for millions of young people.

CARRIED AWAY

Dead in sin, our generation is being carried away from our rightful place of inheritance and authority. The young man in LUKE 7 could have grown to become a respected figure in his city but his life was cut short and his destiny and authority

never realized. Sexual compromise has the same effect on destiny and authority. The lives of countless young men and women are dictated by the opinions and ever changing ideals of a deteriorating culture. In allowing themselves to be effortlessly carried by such ideals, they bypass God's original plan for their lives.

The fact that the young man in Luke is being carried away from the gates of the city is significant because the gate represents authority. It is God's intention that you live with and walk in authority. Sometimes we put up with things in life that we have been given the authority to cast out. Your tolerance may be a result of the fact that your authority has been diluted through impurity and compromise. Lack of purity affects intended influence. **The truth is that you do not have to be a product of the culture.** Choose to stand up and take the authority you have as a follower of Christ.

It takes only moments of exposure to the super sexualized media to sense the surging current attempting to carry you past your principles. The first time I saw any images of pornography I was on vacation with my family, flipping through the channels in a hotel room trying to find a basketball game. The Golden State Warriors were playing and I couldn't wait to see Chris Webber in his rookie season. But during my search for the game, I came to the hotel's preview channel for pornography. I couldn't believe the images in front of me. There I was, 13-years old, trying to watch basketball — bombarded by porn. If we do not fight

for our footing in the area of purity, we are doomed to be swept past the teachings of the Bible — destined to abandon conviction and be carried by compromise. The truth is, I left the TV on that channel a few moments longer than I should have. That night as I went to sleep, I couldn't believe what I had done. I wish I would have gone to my Dad and told him about it, but I felt too guilty about seeing something I didn't even mean to view. Jesus is the only answer to the onslaught of perversion we witness everyday. He has come to help us overcome in the midst of our culture.

↳ *Judah at his 13th birthday — got a Bible*

A GENERATION OF DESTINY

When Jesus shows up in the city of Nain it is actually the tears of a crying mom that capture His attention and cause Him to stop for the funeral. Jesus is moved by tears shed on behalf of a younger generation.

I believe there is a preceding generation crying because they are grieved by the state of today's youth. They are asking "What can we do?" while shedding tears as they attempt to redirect youth away from the compromise they had engaged themselves in. Thank God somebody is praying. This unnamed young man in **LUKE 7** is the only son of his mother and the only hope she has of carrying on her legacy. Young people consumed with Christ and His convictions are the only hope for tomorrow's church and tomorrow's world.

In order to understand the importance of your purity, you must realize that currently only 4% of teenagers in America (born after 1984) consider themselves Bible-based believers.[1] **Your purity isn't just about you.** Your decisions have widespread influence and your compromise is hurting the future of your nation! You may think you are just flirting; just having fun; checking something out late at night, having no idea that, by your actions or inaction, you have abdicated your God-given authority. Generational patterns are established when you make Godly decisions for your life.

We are the church — the hope of the world. I believe we will take our rightful place of authority and our influence will change the course of cities and the lives of others around us. Last fall while preaching at a youth conference I was inspired by a 15-year old young man on a personal mission to end slavery around the world. His cause, Change to Loosen Chains, increases awareness of slavery and sends funds to reputable organizations to stop the human slave trade. Last summer alone Zach Hunter spoke to hundreds of thousands of students in many different nations to increase awareness of the problem. He is taking his place of authority. What is yours?

SIT UP

Back to our story. Here is Jesus having just interrupted the funeral in Nain. He grabs the boy's open coffin and declares boldly, "Young man, I say to you arise!" There is stillness for a moment. I bet everyone is thinking, "He did not just say that." You know what I love about this passage? The Bible says the boy is in an open coffin. Some of you think you've blown it and your destiny is signed, sealed and delivered. You may feel like there is nothing you can do to escape the situation you have gotten yourself into. The truth is that there is hope for you. We serve the God of the open coffin. We serve the Savior of the open tomb. It doesn't matter how far you've strayed or what disease you've transmitted. If we confess our sins God is faithful to forgive and purify us (1 JOHN 1:9). If God can resurrect a body, He can heal it too. He can take you out of a place of desperation and compromise and restore you to His purposes.

A friend I went to Junior High with, Andy, has the most amazing story of God restoring his life after he messed it up. This is how he tells the story:

I lived for myself most my life, caught in the desires of things and feelings. I started drinking in 8th grade. I was by myself in the beginning but quickly found older groups to hang with that drank and smoked. I became a teenage alcoholic, which was normal from my perspective. I met a girl I went to High School with at a party. All of us in the group went through phases of drug use. Some made it out, some didn't. We did, but kept the lifestyle and the drinking. All the time we were dating and sleeping together our relationship was pretty shaky. We got into a lot of fights and had lots of problems, but we moved in together as soon as I graduated and she quickly became pregnant. So naturally we got married.

↳ *Andy in High School.*

I worked as much as I could to try and buy the latest and greatest stuff, neglecting my family and falling deeper into alcoholism. We seemed to be successful, had a beautiful son, bought a house, had four cars, a boat, hot tub, four wheelers, parties every weekend sometimes every night, living the dream. All the while my life was falling apart behind my back. My wife of four years left me for another guy who had just a little bit more stuff than me and paid a little more attention to her than I did. She was pregnant with his son while still married to me. I thought I had it all but in an instant it was all ripped away. The same thing that brought us together tore us apart. I have never felt, or can describe the feeling and pain of divorce. In many cases I feel it's worse than death. The reality of the situation hit me so hard, my life didn't work. It failed. All that I had done and worked for ended in pain.

At that point God came to me. He came to me at the ugliest time of my life. I didn't want God, but He wanted me. He chased me, with hope and deliverance and with people. I gave up, gave in and gave it all away. I asked God to help me, I couldn't do it on my own and I didn't want this life anymore. The next morning I woke up with the desire and hunger to drink completely gone, overnight! It was a miracle. The desire to drink had been with me most of my life. You can die for quitting drinking that fast. The Lord healed me. The story of my life since then has been that of restoration and God-directed right choices. God has redeemed the time in my life.

My mom invited me to dinner on a Wednesday night. On our way we decided to go to Generation Church instead. As soon as I stepped foot in the sanctuary I felt the presence of God like never before. My life was forever changed. I made a commitment to God that I would fully follow Him in every area of my life, and He would restore me. Over the next four years **God supernaturally rebuilt my life**. I got plugged into the best church and small group that helped grow my relationship with God. I can't believe the people He surrounded me with. Through the Word, prayer and obedience to the pastors and leaders speaking into my life, I found the right way to live; God's way. It took years to wash my mind of the foul life I was accustom to, but with God's grace I lived a life of higher standards and purity set apart for His purpose and His will for my life.

When it came time for me to date again, I didn't want my old life to happen again and step out of all of what God had done for me. I wanted to do it right, God's way. I wanted to live the same

Andy & Kacee with Cameron.
↳

life of consecration while dating and in marriage. I prayed and asked God to bring my wife into my life. The one He had for me, and I would wait for her. Soon after that prayer God picked the apple from the top of the tree for me. The most beautiful, holy, anointed woman of God started hanging out with me and my friends. She was on staff at GC and practically a pastor. I thought that only pastors could date pastors. I looked up to her as a leader and admired her love for God and people. I thought more than once, "How in the world can a guy with a past like mine ever get to date such a gift of a person as Kacee?" My chance to be around her came after staying late at a GC service, a few of us would be left including Kacee and we would all go out to Red Robin to eat. I started to really like Kacee, but I waited

a long time to get her phone number. We always hung out in groups. When she invited me to a Christmas party I realized she had feelings for me too and God was about to answer my prayer.

First I asked her dad. Then I asked our Senior Associate Pastor, and my pastor. They all said yes! I could go on a date! The first time Kacee and I were alone was going to dinner four months after we started hanging out. It was amazing and right. God continued to bless and grow our relationship. Kacee and I agreed to not get physical but to continue to get to know one another. We didn't want to compromise our destiny. Kacee and I found out that we are so right for one another in so many ways and it is truly a divine fit. At summer camp I asked God to speak to me about marrying Kacee. It turned out after camp God had spoke to both of us, and soon after I asked Kacee to be my wife. She said yes! Not once during our nine months of dating did we cross the line. We honored God with our relationship. God blessed our engagement, our wedding and our honeymoon in everyway possible. It was the most beautiful process of my life. My son Cameron loves Kacee and family has been restored to my life. We all go to church on Sunday as a family now. I can hardly believe how good my life is because of the grace and mercy of God. He truly pulled me from the mire and set me on a rock. He has blessed me beyond what I imagined. She is my reward for doing it right.

No matter what your journey has been up to this point, God can put you back in the place of influence He has for you. The moment Jesus spoke into the coffin the boy did two things: he sat up and he spoke up. It is time for us to sit up! I believe young people are starting to sit up as God is positioning them in society. God will give us far reaching influence as we learn to be holy and pure. **2 TIMOTHY 2:21** tells us that those who cleanse themselves from impurity are useful to their Master for every good work. So sit up! God knows where you've been. He's familiar with the coffin you've been laying in, but He is calling you to sit up because He knows where He intends to take you. Now is the time to respond in obedience and faith and sit up.

SPEAK UP

After sitting up the young man in the coffin speaks up. The Bible doesn't record what he says because evidently the fact that he speaks up is what is most important. God is looking for a generation who will say something, even if they don't always know exactly what to say. I started to speak up a long time ago and I haven't stopped since. As a senior in high school I stood up in my lunch room, introduced myself, and told the testimony of what God had done in my life. I got a standing ovation. The speech teacher used my sermon for two weeks as an illustration of effective communication. She ended up preaching the gospel over and over. Why? Because somebody spoke up. I wasn't quite sure what to say and I was so nervous it was crazy — but I said something. **I was not willing to remain silent while my peers went to hell.** God wants to use your words to change the lives of people around you who are hungry for truth and in desperate need of Jesus. Say something.

Generation Church currently has 1500 radical students. Every week I go to the Bible and preach the truth about God's plan for their lives. Young people are getting saved around our city. I got word that a three state summit was held by a national abortion organization to discuss teen sexuality. I've been told by Christian representatives from the summit that the leader, a pro-abortion, free sex kind of man, got up on stage and pulled out four pages of notes on me! He told the group he was concerned about a young man in Seattle who is propagating a new youth movement called Generation Church. He accused "this movement" of speaking out against abortion and teenage sex. "We've got to do something about it," he concluded. He had even developed four points on how to combat what we're doing in the lives of

↳ *Judah preaching at Generation Church*

young people in the Northwest. I couldn't believe it! Our voice is being heard as we speak out.

THE BEAUTIFUL AFFLICTION

Just as Jesus restored life and beauty to a family and city that had become afflicted, we need to restore beauty to sex. Sex is beautiful if we are walking in purity, but compromise turns it into torment and affliction — it will either be one or the other.

My passion for purity stems from a process I myself have been through in my relationship with God. As a sixteen year old boy, sick of my sin and the lust in my own heart, I cried out to God saying, "I just want to be holy. I just want to be pure. I don't want to be caught up with the compromise in my generation." At that point I had no idea that one day I would pastor Generation Church. I wasn't aware of the way my current decisions would impact my life and leadership today. I just wanted purity. I wanted to know God and be with Him. Now I look back and realize that this desire led to a defining moment for me. I determined in my heart that I would live pure no matter what it cost.

God met me and I believe He will meet you. I believe you can change your mindsets and the decisions you make. I believe you can find your identity in your Heavenly Father and be motivated by a desire to please Him that dictates the way you live your life. I believe you can live pure.

Chapter 2
MAN WITHOUT MIXTURE

"Safe sex!"

In a public high school, a young man was being asked to define the word "purity." As part of a video survey, peers stuck a camera in his face and, with conviction in his voice, this student proudly declared what he believed to be the answer: safe sex. When I saw the video, I was preparing to preach at a youth conference, and realized that we had more work to do than I thought.

We are part of a generation that does not know the meaning of the word "pure." At sixteen years old I wanted to discover God's

definition of purity so I began a twelve year study that took me from Genesis to Revelation. I didn't do this because I wanted to be known someday as "the purity man," but because I was seeking a biblically based answer to what I believe to be a critical question in our day: What is purity?

It is my passion that after reading these writings you will be able to look directly into a camera and explain, precisely and biblically, what purity is. I shudder at the realization that if I

↳ *Judah, age 16.*

put you on the spot and held a camera in front of your face at this moment, you might stutter and not know the answer to this significant 21st Century question. What is purity? The young man in the video thought that he had the answer. His answer was essentially that purity is using a condom. The propaganda in our culture has twisted the true meaning of real sex and real purity.

WHAT IS PURITY?

In the last chapter we discussed our society's position in regards to God's definition of purity. Now I want to clarify for you what God's definition of purity is. What is purity? Purity is the state of being without mixture. Without mixture!

God's original intention was for man to be without mixture.

Let's imagine a sealed water bottle. The worth of the water is based on its purity. If I were to give you the sealed water bottle I am sure you would have no problem drinking from it. Why? Because it is pure — bottled at the source, sealed, and guaranteed. If I opened the bottle and drank from it, many of the people reading this book would be hesitant to drink after me because the water would have been compromised by my lips. But I'm sure there are plenty of Junior High boys who would still drink it. But what if the water were contaminated even further, what if I added spit or dirt or old milk. No one would want to drink it because it would no longer be pure — no longer consistent with its label. In the same way, our lives are inconsistent with God's original intention because we have been compromised by impurities.

From the beginning of creation, God intended for you to be an individual dedicated solely to His purposes. **GENESIS 1:26** says that God created man

in His image. When God made Adam and Eve in His image He made them completely pure. They were consumed with doing God's will. Unfortunately, we read later in the same chapter that their purity was compromised by the first act of sin, which had to do with the consumption of forbidden fruit in disobedience to the will of God.

MIXTURE ENTERS MANKIND

We have fallen far from God's original plan for mankind. We read in Genesis that sin entered mankind for the first time through the digestion of forbidden fruit. Man's first act of sin was internal. The problem in this case was not the fruit itself, but the fact that as fruit filled the stomachs of Adam and Eve, sin filled the being of man. Man's consumption of the fruit was an act of disobedience and a deliberate decision to give in to self-will rather than God's will. The mixture of self-will with God's will originated with man's choice to do his own thing and the Bible says that from that point on, mixture entered man. Compromised purity resulted in

contamination — a contamination that God is still working to restore.

Adam and Eve's response to mixture was shame. **GENESIS 3** tells us that they ate the forbidden fruit and immediately their eyes were opened, causing them to realize that they were naked. Notice that their compromise immediately affected their sexuality. They went from shameless freedom concerning sexuality to sudden embarrassment and insecurity. Similarly, young people are discovering that the "fruit" which promised ecstasy is leaving them ashamed.

Society will try to tell you that if you eat more forbidden fruit eventually your feelings of conviction will go away. The truth is that the only way to experience maximum sex is to get detoxified. You have to get decontaminated and live the way God originally intended you to — without mixture.

Adam and Eve reacted to their feelings of shame much like young people today — they attempted to cover them up. Realizing they were naked, they made clothes for themselves out of fig leaves. Can you imagine the scene? Adam and Eve were in a garden plucking leaves off trees and trying to position them in strategic places. This is similar to the asinine attempts that people have been making for centuries to recover what has been lost in sin. In our own efforts, we try to make ourselves pure. I can't even count how many young people I have seen try this throughout the years of youth ministry.

A few years back, a student leader in Generation Church "messed up" and made out with a boy she shouldn't have. She confessed right away and felt absolutely horrible! But instead of dealing with the consequences, accepting Jesus' forgiveness and moving on, she lived under continual condemnation and tried to make herself worthy to be a leader. The problem was that she was never worthy in the first place and she could never make herself worthy. Unfortunately, she grew too tired of trying and eventually just gave up and started living for herself. To this day she still isn't walking with God.

The last thing I want you to do after reading this book is think that you are going to "work on your purity" and change the way you live. I have been in ministry long enough to know that you will last about two months before deciding that it is impossible to live a holy life. You gentlemen, who are visually driven, will resolve not to look at anything that might cause you to compromise and will end up averting your eyes and casting down high thoughts everywhere you go. You ladies, who are emotionally driven, will resolve not to fantasize about what it would be like to date that quarterback and how good you would look on his arm. I'm all for looking away and guarding your thoughts but you can't resort to living pure in your own strength.

All of your efforts, young man and young lady, are like Adam and Eve trying to cover themselves with leaves. You might be trying to cover yourself with cool designer leaves or multicolor leaves. It's still just leaves. Stop trying to make yourself holy.

GO AND SIN NO MORE

While some young people attempt to cover their sin, others try to justify it. I meet with students who have bought into the lie that "to err is human" and believe that efforts to live blamelessly are futile. This idea stems from an unbalanced understanding of who Jesus is. People come to me saying that "Jesus is love. He loves everyone the way they are — sexual addictions and all." This is true, but Jesus loves you the way you are so He can make you into the person He wants you to become.

You are probably familiar with the Biblical account of the woman caught in adultery from JOHN 8. Some read that story and focus on the fact that, although the woman was found sleeping with a married man — a crime worthy of death according to Jewish law, Jesus did not condemn her. People bring that story to my attention as a means of proving that "Jesus is all about the love," which He is, but you have to read the end of the story. After assuring the woman that He did not accuse her, meek, mild, kind, compassionate, gracious, all-knowing Jesus instructed her never to do it again. He said "go and sin no more." I bet this woman was thinking "Come on, Jesus. That's easy for you to say. Are you familiar with the family I grew up in? Don't you know how I make a living? Where is the grace?" Does this sound familiar? It is a mistake to think of Jesus as only either grace or judge. Jesus is both.

He is not just the "Lover" of your soul, but also the "Perfecter" of your faith. If Jesus asks us to live free from sin, it must be possible. Be encouraged by the fact that if God commands you to do something He will give you the grace and ability to carry it out.

THE EXPRESSED IMAGE OF GOD

Man without mixture is the expressed image of God. Let's end the chapter with this thought.

As I stated earlier, GENESIS 1:26 records the creation of man, at which time God declared "let Us make man in Our image." God didn't say "let Us make whale, let Us make dog, let Us make tree in Our image," He said "let Us make man." Mankind is the centerpiece of God's creation and the only element of creation that bears His image. Theologians believe that light originally emanated from Adam and Eve because of their pure essence. Unfortunately, they were mixed-up when sin entered their being and God has been working to restore purity to man since that time. This restoration is critical because man without mixture is the expressed reflection of who God is.

Let me explain. GENESIS 22 recounts the well-known story of Abraham's willingness to sacrifice his son, Isaac, to God. At what was undoubtedly one of the most significant moments in his life, Abraham receives these instructions from God: "Abraham, take your only son Isaac to a mountain which I shall show you and sacrifice him there as a burnt offering to Me."

Now you may not understand the full meaning of the term "burnt offering," but Abraham and Isaac did. In the time in which Abraham lived, a burnt offering involved cutting an animal from its throat down to its midsection, ripping it open, gutting out all of its insides, and starting a fire on the inside of the body that would burn the sacrifice from the inside out. The possibility that a parent would agree to sacrifice a child in this way is unimaginable!

Abraham responded obediently to God's request. He and Isaac climbed up the mountain that day, found the spot God guided them to, and started building the altar — a process that would have taken several hours. I can imagine that, while they piled up sticks, Isaac asked his father what the sacrifice would be. Abraham had to explain, likely amidst tears, that his teenage son would be the sacrifice. This man, the father of our faith, tied up his boy, laid him on the altar, and lifted his knife to slay his son when God interrupted at the last moment and told him to stop. Why did God wait so long? Why not stop them after the altar was finished or before he drew his knife? Abraham was a hundred years old at the time, what if he didn't hear God right?! God isn't into human sacrifice, but was looking for His image in Abraham. Two thousand years later, God the Father would offer His son, Jesus, on that same hill. When Abraham lifted his knife, God said "stop, pull away. I see Myself in you. You have gone far enough." The difference was that God would actually go through with sacrificing His son.

God allowed Abraham to undergo a difficult process that was only complete when God's image was clearly reflected in him. When that process was finished, God blessed Abraham more than any other human being that ever lived because He was pleased with what He saw in him — He saw Himself.

It is my prayer that, at some point in my life, God will stop me and say "I see Myself in you." What concerns me is a church that has a message without the image. I am afraid that there are Christians walking around who talk about Jesus but don't look anything like Him. We live among people who are desperate to see Jesus reflected in life lived genuinely. They don't want to hear empty words. Purity extends far beyond not doing wrong, not sleeping with somebody, not watching provocative TV shows. **Purity is the restoration of the image of God in you.** Don't you know you are the only Jesus many people will ever see? In compromising your lifestyle, you forfeit your capacity to accurately reflect God's image and endanger an entire generation's understanding of Jesus.

In the same way, as with Abraham, God wants to walk you through a purifying process and remove the junk from your life so that His nature is reflected to those around you. Paul described this walk as the process of "being transformed into [God's] likeness with ever-increasing glory" (**2 CORINTHIANS 3:18**). God also wants to bless you. You must decrease so that He can increase. You must go to God seeking His divine enablement and invite Him to help you live blamelessly. You must make it a priority to spend time seeking God with the purpose of better understanding His character and allowing His spirit to make you more like Him in your thoughts, attitudes, and actions. King David wrote that he would be satisfied when he bore God's likeness (**PSALM 17:15**). Make a decision never to leave God and ask Him to make you a young person without mixture.

Chapter 3
WHY YOUR PURITY DOESN'T WORK

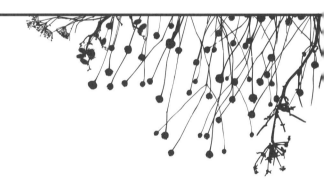

I am not a mechanical kind of guy. I struggle putting my sons' toys together and feel helpless when faced with setting up a high tech, wired machine. I admit that I have had my bouts of inner healing when it comes to my computer and cell phone. I was recently having trouble with my computer and was at the end of my rope. I wanted to drop kick the computer off the Space Needle but resisted the urge and instead handed it over to our resident computer expert, Bryan. I didn't actually want Bryan to fix it. I kind of wanted the computer to suffer. Sad, I know. It took Bryan just a few hours to solve the problem and my computer came back to me a completely different machine — brighter, faster, and more respectful of me as its owner!

I am also baffled by the baby strollers they make these days! Manufacturers must think we have five hands. You have to press and pull five levers at the same time in order to break down the stroller into a size suitable for the car trunk or a plane ride! I once held up a long line of people waiting to get through airport security because I simply do not possess the five hands needed to collapse a stroller. Of course my wife thinks it is easy! She can sip her latte, hold our sons, and talk on her cell phone while pressing, pulling, and pushing to collapse the stroller.

In these instances I had determined that the computer and the stroller were broken. "They just don't work," I would say over and over. I am often convinced that a machine's problem is the fault of the manufacturer but usually find that the machines do work properly, I just don't know how to work them.

↳ *Chelsea pushing Eliott in a stroller*

A lot of people view sexual purity in the same way. They are certain that purity just doesn't work. They may even believe that it works for others but not for them. I want to set the record straight. **You don't have to feel helpless or live in constant frustration in the area of your sexuality.** Purity can work for you; you just need to know how to work it.

I want to share with you the three primary reasons why your purity may not be working. I believe that there are three wrong beliefs young people have about purity:

1.   Seeing purity as a point rather than a process

2.   Living in extremes rather than balance

3.   Seeing defeat rather than disobedience

If you adjust your perspective you can experience life without mixture.

SEEING A POINT RATHER THAN A PROCESS

Seemingly every classic Disney cartoon contains what I call the "Disney Swirl." The Disney Swirl takes place when a beast, a pauper, a puppet, or a plain maid is caught up in a starry swirl and transformed into what they have always dreamed of becoming; a prince or a princess. I think that

many Christians are hoping to experience a Disney Swirl in their pursuit of sanctification. When you come to the cross there is a magical exchange that takes place, but walking out your purity everyday is a process, not magic. Your purity will not work if you view it as a point to arrive at rather than a process to undergo.

I have met with young men who don't make progress in the area of sexual purity because they are subconsciously waiting for a magical moment in which God takes all their sexual desires away. That moment will never come! You are not going to experience the Disney Swirl and will become frustrated looking for it. We live in a fallen world where you have to make a decision to submit to God's will rather than your own every single day. Jesus instructed us to take up our

cross daily. Why? Because purity is not a line we cross, it is a direction we take. You must determine daily to walk out the process of purity.

The Bible mentions the process of refining silver several times. The process of purity is much like the purification of silver. When a silversmith purifies this precious metal he stands attentively over the crucible watching the molten liquid separate. He continually scrapes the dross off the top until finally, after countless hours, he can see his reflection in the silver. At that point the silversmith removes the pot from the fire because the silver has been purified.

PSALM 66:10 says that God tests us like silver refined in a pot. As with the silver, unnecessary stuff will rise to the surface of your life while you undergo the refining process. When junk is revealed you may be inclined to respond with the following thoughts: "Oh, purity doesn't work for me. Look what happened. I'm a pervert. I did it again. I might as well not even try." When you understand the work of God however, you will recognize that stuff coming up is a

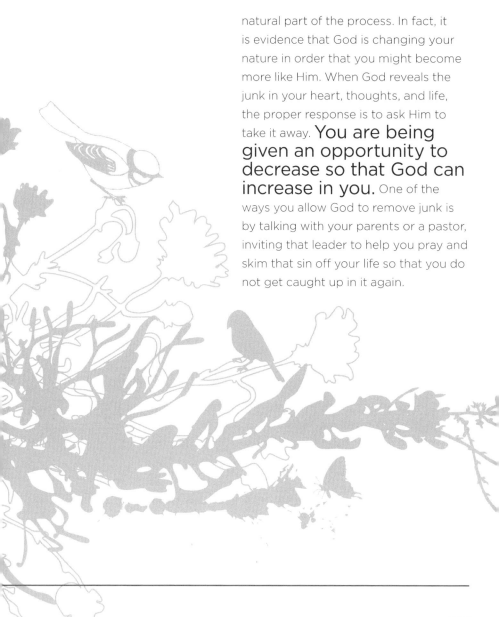

natural part of the process. In fact, it is evidence that God is changing your nature in order that you might become more like Him. When God reveals the junk in your heart, thoughts, and life, the proper response is to ask Him to take it away. **You are being given an opportunity to decrease so that God can increase in you.** One of the ways you allow God to remove junk is by talking with your parents or a pastor, inviting that leader to help you pray and skim that sin off your life so that you do not get caught up in it again.

LIVING IN EXTREMES RATHER THAN BALANCE

People cannot survive in extreme conditions for long periods of time, yet many have adopted extreme views of who Jesus is. There are two extremes we run into when living out our purity: extreme mercy or extreme works. If you try to live in one of these extremes, purity will not work for you.

On one end of the spectrum is extreme mercy. People who take this view tend to believe that God's grace is the constant cover up for all of their sin. They may develop a habit of living for themselves all week, asking for forgiveness on Sunday, and starting the cycle all over again on Monday. They defend the idea that God loves them just the way they are, twisting this truth to justify their lack of motivation to live according to Biblical standards. I usually meet at least one young person who fits this description at every church conference I attend.

Several years ago, while preaching at a youth conference, I felt God tell me that someone in attendance had a marijuana pipe with them. I stood on the platform that night and invited that person to respond to the Holy Spirit. Sure enough, a young man raised his hand and joined me up front. Before praying for this man, I asked him to give me his pipe, believing that God was going to set him free. His response to my request was shocking. He said, "What do you mean? I'm closest to Jesus when I smoke my pipe." His perspective was that God simply loved him the way he was. God does love that young man, but He was trying to give him the opportunity and grace to change. Instead of using the

excuse of extreme mercy, we must access God's grace, His empowering to live the life He asks of us, not a big cover up.

The flip side of extreme mercy is extreme works. The extreme works person thinks that if he strives, wears Christian t-shirts, prays a lot, hangs out with the right people, and eliminates forms of media, he can make himself pure. Rather than living in obedience to God, his actions are dictated by his own desperate attempts to be holy.

You cannot survive in either of these extremes for any length of time. The all-mercy guy is bound to find himself living carelessly and involved in gross sin. The all-works guy will end up discouraged, disillusioned, and exhausted, believing that he will never be able to meet the demands placed on

him by Christian leaders. Either way, the end result is the same. Both people end up leaving the church and giving up on their pursuit of purity.

Discovering a balance between mercy and works is as simple as acting in obedience to the things God asks of you. In his letter to the Philippian church, Paul writes:

"Therefore my beloved, as you have always obeyed not as in my presence only but now much more in my absence, **work out** *your own salvation with fear and trembling. For it is God who* **works in** *you both to will and to do for His good pleasure"* —**PHILIPPIANS 2:12**

Paul instructs Christians to rely on God, not their own ability, while working out their salvation. Your commitment to live according to Biblical principles, submission to the authority of godly leaders, and daily obedience to the Spirit of God operating on the inside of you will enable you to live a blameless life.

SEEING DEFEAT RATHER THAN DISOBEDIENCE

I cannot count the number of times young people have told me that they are being "defeated" by the devil. In making this claim, they subtly escape personal responsibility for their lifestyle choices. They give some entity outside of themselves credit for making them sin. My Bible says that "I can do all things through Christ who strengthens me" (**PHILIPPIANS 4:13**). My God is bigger than the devil, therefore he has no power to defeat me.

The concept of defeat should be called what it is: disobedience. When you mess up you ought to admit your decision to sin in deliberate disobedience to God's will. It would be so refreshing if someone came up to me and said, "Judah, can you pray for me? I've been so disobedient. I've been choosing to sin against God, my mom, my dad, and you as my Pastor." Once you are willing to make the distinction between defeat and disobedience, and take responsibility for your choices, you are on the road to making purity work for you.

While I still have no idea how to fix a computer, I have learned a thing or two about strollers lately. You should see how coordinated I am folding down the stroller with one hand as I hold Zion's hand and keep Eliott from running off all at the same time. I can see other dads look at me thinking, "How does he do that?" I know how to work a stroller! As you learn how to work your purity other people who want to be pure will ask you how you do it.

Chapter 4
CROUCHING, CRAVING, CHASING

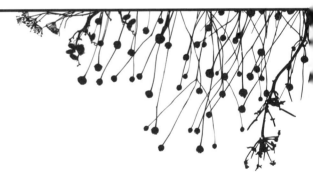

Spending an afternoon at home several months ago I heard
a knock on the front door. I answered the door to find two
unassuming gentlemen who asked me if I would like to buy
something. Having no concept of all that would ensue, I
somewhat ignorantly asked the men what they were selling.
In answer to my inquiry, the salesmen rapidly began to
unload a box of beef. Before I knew it, the foyer of my house
was lined with vacuum packed steaks. There must have
been at least two cows worth! I was overwhelmed! As the
salesmen provided me with a detailed description of each
cut of beef, I began to panic and called for my wife. I have a
hard time resisting when I'm pressured to buy something. I
retreated to the kitchen while Chelsea listened to the sales
pitch. The men were trying to convince her to buy the meat
with statements like: "If you buy this one we'll add another for
only $19.99. In fact, we'll give you a free one for only $9.99."
Free? $9.99? What?

As I hid-out, huddled in the kitchen, the men continued.
"These are the best steaks you can buy. They're straight from
Nebraska. We vacuum packed them ourselves. Some have
even been marinated. If we don't sell them we might not be
able to put food on the table for our families. This is how we
make a living and so far none of your neighbors have bought
anything. We'd like to make you a very, very good deal." All
the while I was in the other room thinking, "Come on Chelsea,
just buy some steaks," but my wife continued to tell the men
that we were not interested.

The sales pitch continued. "We have three boxes here but you don't have to buy all of them. Why don't you buy two boxes and we'll throw in a third box for free."

"I'm sorry, we're not interested."

"I completely understand. You guys probably don't want that many steaks. Just buy one box and we'll give you two extra steaks, free of charge."

"No. I'm sorry. We're just not interested."

This conversation went on for at least thirty minutes until finally my wife agreed to buy three steaks just to get rid of the salesmen.

SIN ISN'T A VENDING MACHINE

I used to think that sin was like a vending machine, in which you could deposit money and make a selection: lust; lying; cheating; debauchery; lasciviousness. I thought that sin, desire, and temptation could be released at the press of a

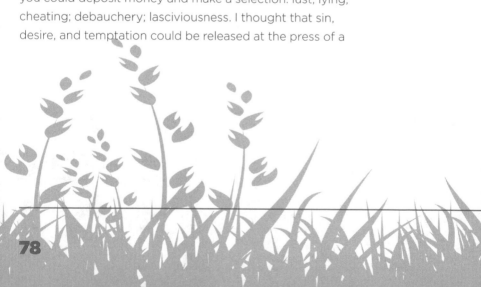

button. I taught young people that these big bad vending machines were everywhere, always wanting their money.

This understanding of the nature of sin was wrong. **GENESIS 4:7** says that "sin lies at the door and its desire is for you." Sin is not a vending machine. Have you ever had a vending machine follow you around during school asking "Do you want a Snickers? Do you want a Snickers? Snickers satisfies." No! Vending machines are stationary. Some are very alluring. Many have codes like C2 or E6 and isn't it a bummer when you press E7 instead of E6 and end up with a granola bar with almonds and dates rather than the Snickers you were craving? The worst is when you press E7 to get your Snickers but it isn't released and ends up dangling by its wrapper. At that point you look both ways and start shaking the machine but it still won't cough up the candy bar.

Sin is not a vending machine. You don't choose to simply walk around sin or keep your distance from it in order to avoid temptation. Sin is more like the men who came to my house selling steaks — it does not take 'no' for an answer.

If sin were selling meat, the conversation would sound something like this:

"I'm sorry. I'm not interested."

"Oh, I totally understand. Why don't you buy one box instead of three?"

"I don't want any steaks."

"Okay, here's what I'll do. I'll give you three steaks at an incredible price. I'll even throw in two for free."

"No, thank you."

"This is Nebraska beef. It's vacuum packed. It's been marinating for thirty-five years."

"Wow. I don't think I'm interested."

"I'm going to give you the best deal you've ever had."

Sin is like that. Sin will pursue you aggressively.

THE NATURE OF SIN

The way you relate to and overcome sin changes when you understand its nature. In **GENESIS 4** God tells Cain that sin lies at his door. This statement may give you the impression that sin lies around waiting to be engaged and is at your disposal. You think "Well, if I want to sin I'll do it a little bit and then get back to living the Christian way." If this is your philosophy, you don't realize that sin has a life and agenda of its own.

Sin is mentioned in the Bible for the first time in **GENESIS 4:7**. It is important to note the first mention of a Biblical concept because it often reveals the significance of a word or principle that is taught throughout scripture. When sin is introduced in Genesis its nature is described. The Bible says that sin *lies*. The word *lie* means "to crouch". Do you know what a crouching position looks like? An animal crouches when preparing to pounce. The whole point of crouching is pouncing. God goes on to say that "sin is crouching at your door and it desires you." You must realize that sin is crouching at your door with plans to pounce on you, control your decisions, and destroy your life.

Sin has an aggressive nature. Throughout the book of Proverbs, the crafty harlot is referred to as a metaphor for sin. The crafty harlot is aggressive! Her feet will not stay at home; she catches and kisses ignorant men; she initiates and pursues. Sin is so aggressive that you don't have to seek it out. Have you noticed that in this day and age you don't have to look hard to fall morally? You can compromise your sexual purity anytime and anywhere. You can compromise your sexual purity in church if you have a cell phone. Sin wants to possess you.

If you are not aggressive in the pursuit of God and purity, you are at the disposal of sin. ROMANS 6:16 says that you are a slave to whomever you obey, be that sin which leads to death or obedience which leads to righteousness. Is it possible to be a slave to a vending machine? No. Sin pursues you in an attempt to become your master.

TAKING DOMINION OVER SIN

When talking with Cain, God describes
the nature of sin and our relationship to
it. He explains that "sin lies at the door...
but you should rule over it." God has
given you divine legal right to control
and be master of sin — not the other
way around. This is great news! The
next time you are tempted to sin you
don't have to give in, thinking "Oh no.
Here it comes. It's happening again.
My addiction. The same sin I can never
overcome." It is critical that you know
who you are. You have the God-given
authority to resist temptation and take
dominion over sin.

THE PURSUIT OF PURITY

Because sin is aggressive, your purity
must be progressive. Up to this point
I have defined purity as, "the state of
being without mixture." My concern
with this definition is that it may cause
you to view purity as a final destination.
In reality, purity is a process — a
process in which you pursue a life free
of mixture. Purity that is passive is

his life journey to two events: a fight and a race. Does that sound passive to you? In making this comparison Paul is describing pursuit. Every day of his life Paul fought the enemy, resisted the devil, and pursued God. Your pursuit of purity should look the same.

GIVE NO PLACE TO SIN

If your purity lacks pursuit, you will be overtaken by the aggressive sin in our culture. Sin is crouching at your door and all it needs to enter your life is a crack. If you are not busy pursuing God and His purposes when sin knocks, you will eventually open the door.

In **EPHESIANS 4:27** Paul warns Christians not to give the devil a foothold. Many young people mistakenly think that they can flirt with sin and recover. They believe that they can experiment with sin and escape its full consequences. The truth is that sin has a hostile nature and any involvement with it will lead to destruction.

not purity at all. We live in a culture in which sin is pursuing you, therefore you must deliberately pursue purity daily, mature in faith, and grow in intimacy with God. You cannot be passive and be effective.

The Apostle Paul sums up his life using these familiar words: "I have fought the good fight, I have finished the race, I have kept the faith" (**2 TIMOTHY 4:7**). Paul, who is arguably one of the greatest Christians to ever walk the planet, likens

Have you heard about Siegfried and Roy in Las Vegas who performed with white tigers? The men performed more than 30,000 shows with the tigers without complication then all of a sudden, during a show, the 380 pound tiger got out of his routine and pounced on his trainer, Roy. The tiger then clamped his powerful jaws around Roy's neck and dragged him 30 feet offstage like a ragdoll. Roy miraculously survived, but everyone was shocked, claiming that the tiger went crazy. People all over America questioned how a tiger could do such a terrible thing. Another animal trainer after watching the incident concluded "Even though they're raised in captivity and they love us, sometimes their natural instincts just take over.[2]" In reality, the tiger was simply following its instincts and acting according to its nature. The tiger went tiger!

Many of you have a similar view of sin. You think you can control your "pet sin" and you won't suffer the consequences. You think that because you haven't been caught yet you never will. Don't be deceived. Sin is just waiting for the most opportune time to pounce and bring you down. You are stunned and ashamed by the results of your actions but you cracked open the door of your life to temptation. Sin is nothing to flirt with.

FLEE YOUTHFUL LUSTS

2 TIMOTHY 2:22 provides the following instructions for dealing with sexual temptation: "flee youthful lusts." The fact that there is an entire Bible verse addressing how to deal with the cravings of a young person indicates the intensity of the cravings. Your cravings can get you into a very sticky situation.

We have all read Biblical accounts of men and women who stood steadfastly against enemies, boldly faced their opponents, and conquered victoriously in battle. In the face of sexual temptation and compromise however, Paul makes it clear that you are to run. Run! If you are in an environment that is fostering your insatiable appetites and desires — run! When confronted with a situation where you are tempted to compromise sexually — run! Run screaming from the building.

Here is an example of a time when someone should have run:

"Judah, um, I need to talk to you."

"What's going on?"

"I just can't believe it. I did something really bad. There's this girl. We're both Christians and we love God and everything. We were doing a Bible study and...before I knew it...my hands were where they shouldn't be. It's horrible, I know!"

"You suddenly touched her there? Wow. Were you sitting in the front row of the church on Sunday morning or in the middle of a small group meeting? When did it happen?"

"Well, no, um... her parents said it was cool if I came over because we were doing some school work. Then we wanted to talk about your message from last week because it was so good. So I started reading the Bible and I was like "man, check this verse out." So we both just really got into that one verse you shared last week and before I knew it, I looked up and she looked over. And it just seemed like the perfect timing. Now I know I shouldn't have done it."

I have mentioned the fact that many people in this type of situation might offer the following explanation for their actions:

"The devil is totally attacking me, you know what I mean? He pretty much made us kiss. Man. I don't even remember moving in for the kiss. It was just like...boom! You know? Oh my gosh! Demons!"

No, it was you — you went over to her house. The Bible says run.

Let's say that in a lapse of good judgment you decided to visit the house of someone of the opposite sex to whom you were attracted. Let's say that you went up to their bedroom to look at a signed poster of their small group leader. Let's say you ended up opening a Bible and sharing scriptures with one another. **The Bible says run!** About the time when you both lean in to look closely at Malachi 3:3 you should say "This is bad. Gotta go!" Run doesn't mean "Hey girl, I'll call ya later," then slip out the door. Run means run!

Can you imagine what it would be like if you had some friends over and one of them took off running out the door? The next day at school when you asked them to explain their actions they would answer that they felt some youthful cravings coming on. Let's obey scripture at all costs.

FLEE AND PURSUE

It's a good thing **2 TIMOTHY 2:22** doesn't end with the word "flee." If it did we would all be running around randomly, finding ourselves in the same situations over and over again. The scripture says "...flee youthful lusts, but..." Flee but. A lot of people start fleeing but don't know where they are going. "...flee but pursue..." **The best fleeing is good pursuing.** In other words, the best defense is a good offense. God designed you to play offense with your purity. Because sin is not a vending machine, just saying "no" to temptation isn't a strong enough defense.

The greatest deterrent to sin is the pursuit of vision. You need a vision for your life that propels you beyond momentary pleasures; a purpose that causes you to see past temptation to its consequences and compels you to choose righteousness because of its reward. Pursue God. Pursue His purpose. Pursue His plan for your life.

PARTNERS IN PURSUIT

This verse goes on to say "...flee, but pursue... with..." There are no Rambos in the church of Jesus Christ. A decision to seek God and pursue purity on your own will set you up for failure. The Bible instructs you to "flee the evil desires of youth but pursue...with those who call on the Lord out of a pure heart." You want to be pure? Spend time with pure people. You want your good morals corrupted? Hang out with immoral people. Who are your friends? There's a reason we have small groups in Generation Church. Groups of young people meet throughout our region with the purpose of encouraging one another in their pursuit. You need to run alongside someone who is running in the same direction you are.

We are not in a war that will be won with grenades, tanks, or nuclear weapons — we are in a much more diabolical war. We are in a moral war. Not one of us can say that we have never been affected by the war. We have all endured scrapes, bumps, and bruises. We have all failed in one area or another. There may come a day, not long from now, that you lay wounded on the battle field of this moral war in need of a friend to pick you up. You need more than just a pastor who talks to you from a pulpit once a week. You need somebody in your life who knows your first, middle, and last name, who knows what you like and don't like, and who sees you when you're down and when you're up. There may be a moment in this moral war when you experience a bullet wound or, dare I say, even a mortal wound that has the potential to destroy you. Laying on the battle field ready to give up, you think to yourself, "I can't go on. I can never be pure. I don't think I'm going to come to church anymore." It is at that moment when you need a friend who refuses to leave you in defeat and is willing to carry you on their back to safety; someone who is committed to helping you receive God's forgiveness and experience restoration; someone who believes that you can live pure.

"Flee youthful lusts but pursue...with those who call on the Lord out of a pure heart." You've got to do this. **You've got to find a peer who shares your passion for purity.** You have to establish a relationship with a pastor or mentor who is committed to leading you and investing in you. Find someone who will challenge you when you're lagging behind as the troops are moving on.

↳ *Judah & Krist
in 1995*

I have pursued the purposes of God for my life with my cousin and best friend, Krist Wilde. In High School most of our dreams centered around basketball and who could score the most points. But once and a while we dreamed about preaching and pastoring. In both cases we were going after something together, pushing each other to become better. I know in many ways my friendship with him has kept me from doing anything stupid. I realized I wouldn't want to face him and admit what I had done. Who are you running with?

Chapter 5
THE WAY OF ESCAPE

Am I the only one who is insulted by the preflight routine
on an airplane? You know the drill. The flight attendant gets
on the PA and announces, "At this time we would like to ask
you to give us your full attention. If you're reading a book
or a newspaper please put it down for a moment and listen
closely as we guide you through the emergency procedures
for this flight." Have you ever really watched as the flight
attendant shows you how to use the plane's safety devices?
Maybe you have even gone one step further and picked up
the safety information card. I realize that it's necessary for
the airline to provide the card but it all seems redundant. I
have actually been on plane rides where people raised their
hands and asked questions, to which the flight attendant
responded, "Yes? I see that hand." I admit that I don't pay
attention to the safety demonstration or read the card. Call it
pride, boredom, or disinterest.

While flying with my cousin, Jery, he actually took the info
card out of the seat pocket and started reading it. When he
did this I was thinking, "Jery, are you kidding me? Put that
away. People are gonna think you're a new flyer!" Once we
started looking at it though, we couldn't put it down. It is
hilarious! The graphics on the card are state of the art. There
is a picture of an airplane floating in the middle of the Pacific
Ocean with people calmly jumping out of the emergency
exits onto a huge yellow slide. It almost looks like Disneyland.
The slide turned into a raft and the passengers seem so
pleased to be stranded in the middle of nowhere with nothing
more than their ginger ale and life jacket.

While passengers are supposedly looking, the friendly flight attendant positions themselves in the front of the plane and demonstrates the correct way to buckle the seatbelt. "Now to buckle your seatbelt," she begins, "please insert the metal piece into the metal handle." Good thing they cleared that up because most of us were just planning on tying it across our waist. The attendant continues, "Now to release the buckle lift up on the metal tab." Again, good thing they explained this because we were going to bite it in an attempt to tear it off with our teeth. Folks, if you've been in a car since 1965 you can get out of a seatbelt in an airplane. Has it ever dawned on you while the plane is in the air that if something were to go wrong you actually wouldn't know what to do? Sometimes I sit in exit rows and the flight attendant will ask me if I am willing and able to perform the functions outlined on the safety card. When you fly it's culture not to watch the demonstration or read the pamphlet, but the thought of not having an escape plan is unnerving.

↳ *Judah with the*
skateboard his dad
custom-made for him

The neighborhood I grew up in was not the nicest one in the city. On my street, a house was considered upscale if the bars on the windows were painted the same color as the trim. I have to admit that my house had the nicest bars on the whole block. The biggest, toughest gang in my neighborhood was called "Johnny's Gang." Pathetic, I know. They were a skateboard gang.

One afternoon some of the members of Johnny's Gang were skating down my street in the direction of my home. As a brave, strong, 11 year old, I was standing outside of the house and decided that I was going to call the guys the worst name I could think of: Posers! **I liked to stir things up as a kid.** As I perfected my plan, I developed an escape strategy in my mind. It is amazing what you will do if you know your way of escape. As the skateboarders came nearer, I rehearsed my plan. I would shout out the insult, run down

the alley next to my house, and leap over an eight foot fence
at the edge of the property. As they approached, I waited
for the perfect moment and yelled "Posers!" I have to explain
that I was a skinny kid with bleach blonde hair. You have
never seen a scrawny little white dude run so fast! I launched
over the fence and landed right on my face but I had done it!
I had called Johnny's guys posers! For the next two weeks I
bragged to all the kids in the neighborhood about what I had
done.

ALWAYS A WAY OF ESCAPE

You will do crazy things when you know there is a way of
escape. The Bible says that there is a way of escape for
every temptation you will face as a Christian. **1 CORINTHIANS
10:13** promises that "no temptation has overtaken you except
such as is common to man; but God is faithful, Who will not
allow you to be tempted beyond what you are able, but
with the temptation will also make the way of escape, that
you may be able to bear it." Your ability to resist
temptation is dependent on God's
faithfulness in providing an escape
route. Peter assures us that "the Lord knows how to
deliver the godly out of temptations" (**2 PETER 2:9**). When God
says He will give you an exit, He will give you an exit.

You must recognize that, no matter what temptation you face, you are not alone. Not one of us is exempt from being tempted. Even Jesus, our Lord and Savior, was tempted in every point, as we are tempted. You don't have license to defend your behavior with the excuse that no one else has been in your situation or experienced your temptation. At some point we have all come up with various justifications for our inability to find the exit in a tempting circumstance, but there is always a way of escape. This should give you confidence when discussing temptation. God assures you that, come hell or high water, no matter the severity of your circumstance, situation, temptation, allurement, or seduction, He will provide an exit sign. There will always be an opportunity to say "no"; to resist temptation, to run! If I can give you the tools you need to overcome temptation you can experience success in your pursuit of God and holiness on a daily basis.

THE NATURE OF TEMPTATION

It is important for you to understand that temptation itself is not sin. Temptation is an opportunity to sin that is presented by the devil. Giving in to temptation will lead to destruction but temptation is not sin until it mates with your desire. James explains that man is tempted when he

is drawn away by his own desires and "desire conceived gives birth to sin" (**JAMES 1:13-15**). The enemy preys upon your desires and presents you with tempting opportunities. He cannot read your mind but he can make assumptions about your weaknesses based on your lifestyle. He uses these observations to create seductive ploys that capitalize on the desires demonstrated in the way you conduct yourself. When you are attracted to what he's selling and give into sin, he gains a foothold in your life.

Jesus said that Satan had nothing in Him, meaning that there was nothing Satan could offer that He wanted (**JOHN 14:30**). God wants you to get to the same place. If you don't desire that with which you are being tempted, then sin has no power over you. I will never forget the night my youth pastor, Pastor Jude Fouquier, confessed to us his secret obsession. He admitted that he waited until his whole family went to  bed to start looking for it, smelling it out, searching the house for...smelly poopy diapers?!? "What?" our entire youth group shouted back at him as he pulled a poopy diaper from behind the pulpit. He then began eating it! We were shocked! Why was this so hard to believe? Nobody is tempted to eat poopy diapers because nobody has a desire for them. I was relieved to later find out that he was only eating crunchy peanut butter, but the lesson stayed with me. You won't be tempted to consume things you don't desire.

↳ *Pastor Jude preaching, 1992.*

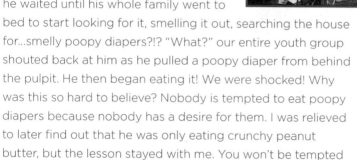

If I can teach you to find the way of escape in times of temptation then Satan cannot influence you. At this point, the enemy may have a patented move that always works on you; the same ploy he uses to bring you to a place where your desire gives birth to sin time and time again. Until you learn to recognize the escape route, you will be caught in a cycle of repenting, asking for forgiveness, and buying into what the devil is selling. Let's explore what the Bible teaches about the way of escape through the life of Joseph.

JOSEPH'S STORY

Joseph was one of the twelve sons of Jacob written about in the book of Genesis. Joseph found himself in a situation that seemed hopeless but made a decision to run from temptation — a decision that ultimately determined his destiny and changed the course of an entire nation.

Joseph was a dreamer. As a young man he had two dreams in which people and things were bowing down to him.

Joseph shared his dreams with friends and family members who eventually got tired of hearing about his future plans to rule over them. Do you have an annoying little brother or sister? Joseph unintentionally became one, and as a result his brothers devised a plan to get rid of him — they were skeptical of the destiny he claimed and jealous of the fact that he was their father's favorite son. They sold Joseph into slavery to the Ishmaelites, who auctioned him off to Potiphar, one of the highest ranking servants to the Pharaoh of Egypt. Joseph ended up working in Potiphar's house and probably doubted that his adolescent dreams would ever come to pass.

A TEMPTING OFFER

Our story picks up in **GENESIS 39**, where it didn't take long for Potiphar to realize that Joseph was different from his other employees. He was unique; he didn't fit in. In fact, Joseph was successful at everything he did. Potiphar put Joseph in charge of his entire household.

Apparently Joseph was a pretty good looking guy, because the Bible tells us that this woman cast longing eyes at him. Potiphar's wife approached Joseph and said "lie with me." She wanted to have sex with him. This approach is not unlike what we experience in today's aggressive culture. Have you ever heard the old song, "I wanna hold your hand, I wanna hold your hand?" Nobody wants to hold your hand anymore. **We live in a different age where people want to take your innocence; they want to take your virginity.** Instead of "I wanna hold your hand" artists are singing "you and me baby ain't nothing but mammals, let's do it like they do on the Discovery Channel."

The girl who propositioned me in High School sure didn't have intentions of holding my hand. I was innocently sitting in Math class when she came up to me and said, "My friend is having a party at her house tonight. She wanted me to tell you she would have sex with you, if you come." I was shocked! At that point I was just a normal High School student, struggling with math. I wasn't the youth pastor of Generation Church. I wasn't traveling around the world preaching to thousands of students. I wasn't the author of a purity book. Yet all that could have been compromised in one moment of sin. What would have happened to Joseph if he gave in?

Potiphar's wife demanded that Joseph have sex with her but Joseph refused. He understood that to do so would be to take advantage of his position of authority, betray his employer, and forfeit the favor he had received from God. Joseph also feared the Lord, which meant he recognized that God was watching everything he did. If I hung out with you everyday for the next two weeks you would undoubtedly experience the purest two weeks of your life. Suddenly, you would have a desire first thing on Saturday morning to read your Bible instead of playing Xbox. Why? It's called the fear of man. The fear of God is even greater. It is a constant awareness of the fact that God is always watching. Remember that next time you have the opportunity to compromise.

The Bible says that Potiphar's wife didn't give up. She pestered Joseph daily. The devil operates in the same way in your life. **The closer you get to fulfilling your dream, the harder Satan will try to entice you to sin.** This is because the fulfillment of your destiny will lead to the enemy's demise.

THE GREAT ESCAPE

The last time Potiphar's wife approached Joseph he was alone. **PROVERBS 18:1** says that "a man who isolates himself seeks his own desire." People who are isolated are often unable to resist temptation because sin is persistent and will not take "no" for an answer. If you avoid being a part of a small group, the reason may be that you want to do your own thing, seeking your own desire without being held accountable for your decisions. You need a "small group."

This woman waited until Joseph was by himself and took her proposition to the next level. She grabbed his clothing. In that second, Joseph had to make a life-altering decision not knowing that in three short years he would be the second most powerful man in the world.

Some of you think "I'm just a College student, what's the big deal? I'm a sophomore in High School so the things I do now don't really matter in the long run. I can still get it together." In reality, you may be three years away from entering into the place of authority God has prepared just for you. You may be three months away from a defining moment that propels you into His grand plans.

Joseph could have easily questioned the purpose of resisting. He could have thought to himself, "If I say no to this woman who's grabbing my garment, it's going to cost me the job that God has given me. God has given me favor with my employer. I can't just throw it all away." If someone was ever justified in choosing not to take the way of escape, it would have been Joseph. When faced with this circumstance, he chose not to give in to temptation. Potiphar's wife still clinging to his shirt, he left his garment behind and ran from the building.

You may be thinking, "Judah, you mean to tell me that if I'm at a party on Friday night, trapped by two good looking women who are grabbing at my shirt, I'm supposed to wiggle my way out of that? C'mon." That's exactly what I'm telling you. Some of you believe that the way of escape is just going to show up suddenly in the form of a genie from a bottle, ready to escort you to the escape exit. **Often times the way of escape presents itself in the form of the Holy Spirit instructing you to get out of a situation.** It may seem too simple, but your common sense comes from God. If you are thinking, "He's taking his clothes off. I should leave now," that could be your exit.

MODERN DAY GARMENTS

I want to focus on the fact that, in the process of fleeing temptation, Joseph left his garment behind. Was the garment itself sin? No, but it was connecting him to sin. Is television sin? No. Are movies sin? No. Is music sin? No. Is dating sin? No! The Bible doesn't say that any of those things themselves are sin but there are times when you can't save both a garment and your dreams. Sometimes you have to give up a garment in order to preserve your future. Don't be deceived into believing that you can have it all and change the world. MATTHEW 16:26 tells us that a man does not profit if he gains the whole world but loses his own soul. So you've got the clothes; you've got the house; you've got the girls. What if you lose your soul? Is it worth it? Would you rather download a song from iTunes or fulfill the plan God has for your life? I'm not saying that those songs are sin but they may be the garment the enemy is using to pull you down. Like you, Joseph had a decision to make: "I can try to save this garment and lose my dreams. I say leave the garment behind. I'm out!"

GIVE UP THE GARMENT

Last year my wife and I decided to turn off our TV for a season. We did it because we were wasting too much time. I'd be tired when I got home from work and convince myself that what I really needed to do was watch ESPN. I enjoy watching sports, but I ended up spending too much time in front of the television so I left the garment behind. It's not worth it to me. Are there garments you need to let go?

My oldest son was born premature and spent the first two weeks of his life in the hospital. During that time, my wife and I stayed in a hotel next door. Especially tired one night, I began to flip through the channels while I waited for Chelsea to come back from the hospital. As I searched for something to watch I came across the movie channel and ended up seeing a terrible image that made my heart race. I immediately turned off the TV but was horrified by the

↳ *Judah holding Zion, born six weeks early*

fact that something deep within me wanted to switch it back on! I have been in ministry for nine years. I have a license that reads "Reverend Judah Elwood Smith." After twelve years of a consistent devotional life a part of me wanted to watch that show. I probably could have justified another look under the premise that I "needed to get a burden for what young people these days really go through," but instead I instantly dropped the remote. We can attempt to come up with spiritual excuses for sin but what we need to do is let go of garments immediately. When you are tempted to sin, take the way of escape and don't give yourself the opportunity to go back!

DIVINE PROMOTION

After Joseph resisted Potiphar's wife, everything in his life seemed to go from bad to worse. He obeyed God, refused to give in to temptation, and left a nice jacket behind only to find himself in the deepest dungeon in the palace. By that time Joseph was probably convinced that following

his convictions hadn't paid off. Have you ever taken the way of escape but circumstances got worse? So you told your friends "no" and now you're the invisible man at your fraternity? What happens when people mock and isolate you? I have been told by young people, "Judah, I don't think I should have gotten water baptized."

"Why?"

"Things are horrible now."

"What do you mean?"

"I go to parties with my friends and I don't have a good time. It's not fun anymore. I'm frustrated. My friends are mad at me. It's terrible!"

This happens sometimes when you obey God. We used to teach people that if they resisted temptation God would help them score more touchdowns at their football games. The truth is that you may get cut from the team. Think about it. Joseph was in the dungeon with a cup bearer who wouldn't stop talking and a crying baker. Joseph had no idea that he was beneath the palace he would soon rule over. He didn't realize that his exterior demotion was actually spiritual promotion. The day Joseph left Potiphar's house was a day of promotion for him. **The way of escape is actually the way of promotion even in situations where you may initially feel demoted.** Joseph sat in the dungeon for two short years

JUDAH SMITH **DATING DELILAH**

until he was called on by Pharaoh to interpret a dream. In one destiny-defining afternoon he was showered, shaven, deodorized, and rushed into the presence of Egypt's ruler, where his God-inspired interpretation of Pharaoh's troubling dream earned him the position of second in command over the entire nation.

Falling prey to temptation for momentary pleasure is not worth forfeiting your destiny. Like Joseph, you may be only a few years away. Never underestimate the power and potential of taking the way of escape in every temptation you face. Each one of us will face temptation but every time you find the supernatural escape route it becomes easier to resist sin and you move closer to the divine promotion that God has in store for you.

LEAVE IT BEHIND

"Others save with fear, pulling them out of the fire, hating even the garment defiled by the flesh." **(JUDE 23)**

It is likely that God has been speaking to you about a garment in your life that is pulling you down while you have been reading this chapter. Your garment could be a digital machine, a DVD, the television, a relationship, a magazine subscription, a habit, or even a food. If you know that there is a garment in your life that the enemy uses to seduce you to sin, I'm asking you to lay it down. Leave the hobby or habit. Leave the machine! It's simple. Leave it behind.

Chapter 6
DATING DELILAH

Do you believe in angels? Do you believe in demons? The Bible makes it clear that there is an unseen world — a spiritual dimension. Although you may not have ever seen or felt such a realm, this fourth dimension is a greater reality than the one in which you live. The spiritual dimension preceded our present dimension and spiritual forces created our world. EPHESIANS 6:12 explains that "we do not wrestle against flesh and blood, but against principalities, against powers, against the rulers of the darkness of this age, against spiritual hosts of wickedness in the heavenly places." There is a war going on in the spiritual realm — a war over souls. There is a God and there is a devil — both of whom desire your devotion. The challenge is that you can't see the war and many people don't believe in what they cannot see.

Often times the pursuit of purity can get so practical that it lacks spiritual understanding. **Your ability to live pure depends upon your belief in the reality that God is working for you while the enemy is working against you.** I want to discuss the subject of dating from this perspective. Dating doesn't start when you go out on Friday night with Billy, Bob or Susie. Dating begins in the heart.

As a senior in high school, I was proud of the fact that I had never dated. One afternoon I was surprised to hear the Holy Spirit tell me that I was dating someone!

"Lord," I responded, "I'm not dating anybody. You know that. I know lots of girls think I'm attractive, but I'm not dating anybody."

The Holy Spirit said again, "No, you're dating somebody."

"Lord, I'm not dating anybody."

"You are."

"Lord, this is rude. I am not dating anybody!"

"You are."

"Then what's her name?"

"Delilah!"

"Ha! See? I don't even know a girl named Delilah. Who would name their daughter Delilah?"

That brief conversation was all it took for me to realize what God was saying. I had read the account of Samson and Delilah's relationship in Judges 16. I had even preached on the subject. Now the Holy Spirit was dealing with me.

DATING BEGINS IN THE HEART

As I allowed God to search my heart, He began to teach me that dating begins in the heart and not on the day you ask someone out to dinner. I have known young people who are so proud of the fact that they don't date. They tell everyone, "I don't have a boyfriend. Nope. I'm holy. Sanctified. Set apart." Or they say, "I haven't even had sex since I've been saved. I'm walking in perfect purity." These young people walk around expecting to receive a pat on the back. Christians tend to flaunt their virginity and proudly wear their "V" like a superhero. When someone of the opposite sex asks their name they respond, "Whoa, whoa. You don't need to know my name. I'm a virgin!" That's weird. Somewhere along the line virginity became the pinnacle expression of purity among church goers.

If you're a virgin I'm proud of you, but you need to recognize that virginity was not Jesus' ultimate commandment. I'm all for virginity until you get married but Jesus did not instruct His disciples to

go into all the world and make virgins of all nations. In fact, the Biblical standard for purity is higher than just abstaining from sex. I encourage the young people in Generation Church to choose not to date during junior high and high school because dating is an internal issue that goes deeper than physical relations. Dating involves more than sitting in the local diner sipping a strawberry milkshake from one frosty glass with two straws. Dating starts in the heart!

CLEAN HANDS, PURE HEARTS

According to **PSALM 24:4**, God desires that you have "clean hands and a pure heart". There is a lot of talk in the church about clean hands and clean actions, but they should not be the ultimate focus. There are young people walking around flaunting their clean hands but it is possible to have clean hands and a heart that is riddled with lust. This is where things get a little ambiguous. It is here that you can slip into church unnoticed as long as you use your spiritual hand sanitizer before you walk through the doors. This is

where you can sneak in and out of your small group. You can even become a leader with hands that appear spotless but a heart that is a cesspool. It has done you no good if you have appeased those around you externally with clean hands but displeased God internally with an impure heart condition.

*"The Lord does not look at the things man looks at. Man looks at the outward appearance, but the Lord looks at the heart." —*1 SAMUEL 16:7 (NIV)

Clean hands are vital but incomplete. God desires the pure heart of a person who wishes to please Him and is dedicated to His purposes. Clean hands are a natural result of a pure heart. It is for this reason that dating ultimately starts in the heart.

I was preaching the hell out of teenagers at a youth conference in Portland, Oregon. After speaking for an hour on purity, it got back to me that some of the young people in attendance had said that my message didn't relate to them because they hadn't lost their virginity. That ticked me off! Don't tell me that you don't need to hear the message of purity because you go to Christian school or don't go out on dates. Don't skim over this chapter thinking that the subject of dating doesn't apply to you simply because you're not involved in a relationship. Consider that dating is first an issue of the heart.

PURITY IS A HEART CONDITION

The title of this book stems from the story of Samson and Delilah recorded in **JUDGES 16**. What is fascinating to me is the fact that Christians make such a big deal of Samson and Delilah's relationship. Delilah is often portrayed as an incredibly sensual woman and Samson a lust monger. In actuality, there is no mention in Judges of sex between the two yet many have perceived their relationship to be sensual. There is no record of Samson and Delilah holding hands or kissing. The most intimate physical contact they had, which I don't recommend, involved Samson putting his head on Delilah's lap and taking a nap. That's it! Samson and Delilah never exchanged sexual words yet it was at the hands of Delilah that the great champion was destroyed.

Everyone is looking out for the "big nasty" and attempting to avoid the act of sex at all costs. You have to realize that purity is not only about external actions; it is not just about heavy petting or a date gone too far.

Purity is about the heart.

We learn from the life of Samson that it is possible to compromise your purity without so much as touching another person. You can pollute your heart in a pretty clean setting or a seemingly sanctified atmosphere. As a pastor, my primary concern is not whether you lift your hands during worship and take notes from the sermon. I'm not going to inspect your hands to see if they are clean. I want to be sure that you have a pure heart.

GUARD YOUR HEART

Maintaining a pure heart takes work. You have to be deliberate about pursuing purity. **PROVERBS 4:23** instructs you to "guard your heart above all else because it determines the course of your life" (NLT). In this context, the word "guard" means to blockade. Have you ever seen a blockade? If you're in Los Angeles turn on the TV on any given weekend and you'll probably see a high speed car chase on the news. The chase almost always ends in a blockade. There are police cars spanning the width of the freeway, officers standing outside their cars holding shields, and helicopters hovering overhead. That's a blockade! The anchor man tensely announces, "The driver of the stolen vehicle is coming up on the blockade. That oughtta stop him!" Proverbs instructs you to similarly blockade your heart.

The point is not whether or not you are having sex. The main concern is who you have given your heart. In the dusty streets of Jerusalem Jesus challenged Old Testament law with the institution of a higher standard. "You have heard it said under the law that if you sleep with someone that is not your husband or wife, it is sin," Jesus began. "But I say to you this day that if a man looks at a woman and lusts after her he has committed adultery in his heart (MATTHEW 5: 27, PARAPHRASE)." According

to the new covenant, if you have sinned in your heart you're guilty. If we live by Jesus' standards then there's not a virgin among us. Your convictions must go beyond maintaining virginity in your body.

WHO IS DELILAH?

As I said earlier, Delilah didn't want sex. Delilah is an unclean spirit and represents an unclean attitude. **PROVERBS 7** refers to this unclean spirit as "the immoral woman." The word "Delilah" means to bring low; to make feeble; to impoverish. There are spirits just like Delilah operating today. Purity does not relate only to romantic relationships; the aim of purity is sustaining a holy attitude. God is interested in the thoughts that occupy your mind. If you are entertaining unclean fantasies and allowing your heart to be consumed with sensual, self-serving ideas, you are dating Delilah!

WHAT IS DATING?

People sometimes ask me if I am against dating. My answer is 'no'. I'm not against spending time with someone exclusively when the season is right and you have the support of parents and pastors. I'm in favor of getting to know another person with the possibility of discovering the individual you will marry. I do think it is wrong to date, flirt, hold hands, kiss, and mack on a person you have no intention of marrying.

I discourage the Junior High and High School students

in my youth ministry from physically or mentally dating just anybody. Some believe that I set the bar too high but I didn't set the bar. The standards I teach were set up by God. According to Jesus, dating starts in the mind, will, and emotions. Maybe this scenario looks familiar:

Your mom says, "You are not going to date him."

In your head you respond, "Well, I may not go to Denny's with him but every night I'm going wherever I want with him in my mind!"

Dating means to "exclusively entertain something or someone." Samson's relationship with Delilah was emotional rather than physical. His decision to surrender the secrets of his heart to another person created a deep emotional connection that eventually destroyed him.

SAMSON'S SECRET

Delilah knew that she could access Samson's heart if she understood the secret of his strength. She didn't press him every day to sleep with her, but to confide in her the source of his great might. Delilah even questioned Samson's love for her, claiming that since he hadn't divulged his deepest secret, he hadn't given her his whole heart. Notice that she didn't question his devotion because they hadn't had sex. It's not enough to make a determination not to be physically intimate with someone. Delilah desired an emotional connection.

The word "vex" is used to describe the intensity with which Delilah pestered Samson. "Vex" indicates impatience to the point of giving in. Don't buy into the lie that you can't wait. Don't be deceived into believing that you can't save your heart for the right person. The unclean, 'Delilah' spirit will press you to surrender and try to convince you that you can't wait until you get married because you love this person. Don't allow yourself to pour out your heart and talk about things that were only meant to be discussed between a husband and wife. **Be aware when you start to go places in your mind that you should only go when you're married.** If you're not careful you will lose the virginity of your heart.

Samson eventually gave in to Delilah's inquiries. He was probably thinking, "I can't take this anymore. I'm tired of resisting. At least we're not having sex." Samson revealed his secret that, as a Nazarite, he was not supposed to cut his hair because the hair was an outward indication of an inward condition. As long as his hair remained untouched, so did his heart. In what likely seemed like a harmless conversation at the time, the champion yielded the secret of his heart and gave his enemies the tools they needed to destroy him.

SOURCE OF STRENGTH

PROVERBS 20:29 says that "the glory of young men is their strength." Delilah tormented Samson with the purpose of taking his strength. This same unclean spirit is after your strength — the strength that is dependent on the purity of your heart, not the cleanliness of your hands alone.

Shortly after explaining to Delilah the connection between his untouched hair and great strength, Samson woke up from a nap and discovered that his head had been shaved by his enemies. When Samson arose he had the same biceps, triceps, and impressive physique, but he had lost his strength because the purity of his heart had been compromised with the cutting of his hair. Purity is about the heart. Dating is about the heart. Blockade your heart and preserve your strength!

LEAN ON THE CROSS

Fortunately, Samson's story doesn't end there. Samson was overtaken by his enemies, had his eyes gouged out, and was locked in prison, unable to defend himself because his strength had been sapped. As a blind prisoner however, his hair eventually began to grow back. The good news for anyone who has lost the virginity of their heart is that God is able to restore that which has been lost and restore what has been destroyed.

On the last day of his life, Samson was brought into a coliseum to entertain an audience of thousands. As this former champion was led by a small boy, he requested that he be situated between the coliseum's two main pillars.

In a scene that looked very similar to Christ's last hours on earth, Samson endured jeering and mocking while he uttered his last words: "Let me die." These were likely the words that God had desired from Samson his entire life. God wanted Samson to die to himself. His words indicated that he finally understood that we must die to selfish desires to truly live. This is the message of the cross. Samson stood firmly between two pillars, his arms outstretched in the same position Christ would assume centuries later on the cross.

Samson exerted his last bit of strength to knock down the pillars he was leaning on, resulting in the collapse of the entire coliseum, his own death, and the death of his enemies. Samson's literal death symbolizes your necessary death to self. Life is not about you. The most important thing in life is not what you want and your ultimate goal is not having your emotional needs met by other people. **You must surrender your will to God's will everyday.** In order to maintain clean hands and a pure heart it is essential that you recognize and accept the substitutionary work Christ did on the cross; exchange your insufficiency for Christ's sufficiency; and lay down your self-serving, carnal nature.

Samson's problem was that he spent most of his life relying on his own ability and didn't recognize his need to lean on something stronger than himself until it was too late. Similarly, you need to lean on the cross. You cannot trust in your own understanding or ingenuity. Come to the cross daily with this prayer: "God, let me die to wrong desires."

Chapter 7
ANCIENT BOUNDARIES

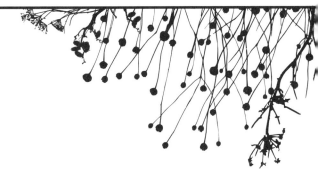

It always surprises me when people think that they can improve on the systems God has established. I heard of a psychologist who thought that the elimination of boundaries would create freedom and promote individuality. In order to prove his theory that limitations stifle growth in children, this man conducted an experiment in which the fences were removed from a recess field at an elementary school. The researcher was sure that confident students who usually attempted to climb the fences and explore beyond school grounds would feel released to wander as they pleased. The results of the experiment were fascinating and unforeseen. When dismissed for recess, the students gathered in a cluster in the center of the recess field. Rather than taking advantage of their new-found freedom, the children experienced feelings of insecurity and uncertainty, and resorted to creating boundaries for themselves. When the fences were restored the very same kids who had huddled together reverted back to scaling fences, testing borders, and utilizing the entire playing field.

Worldly philosophies promote life without boundaries. Many people today argue that there are no absolutes. You have probably heard someone say that "whatever you believe is alright as long as it doesn't hurt anybody". This idea is contrary to Biblical principles. **PROVERBS 22:28** warns, "do not remove an ancient boundary stone set up by your forefathers" (NIV). **Boundaries actually bring security.** Boundaries create freedom. Boundaries provide direction. Boundaries allow you to explore and establish your identity. Boundaries generate purpose.

Ironically, as fences are removed from society in the name of freedom, people become increasingly insecure, misguided, and misdirected.

ABSOLUTE BOUNDARIES

There are ancient boundaries that must be upheld. I am going to identify for you the eight sexual boundaries of the Bible. These boundaries are absolute — they are non-negotiable. If you do not acknowledge and adhere to these boundaries you risk forfeiting God's perfect plan for your life.

BOUNDARY #1: NO SEX BEFORE MARRIAGE

"Finally then, brethren, we urge and exhort in the Lord Jesus that you should abound more and more, just as you received from us how you ought to walk and to please God; for you know what commandments we gave you through the Lord Jesus. For this is the will of God, your sanctification: that you should abstain from sexual immorality; that each of you should know how to possess his own vessel in sanctification

and honor, not in passion of lust, like the Gentiles who do not know God."

—1 THESSALONIANS 4:1-5

There is to be no sex before marriage. **1 THESSALONIANS 4:3** instructs believers to avoid sexually immoral behavior. What does the word "immorality" mean? Immorality comes from the root word "moral," in reference to your morality. Sexual immorality is a misuse of your sexuality. In the case of an unmarried person, sex is considered immoral. If you chose to have sex outside of marriage you will be removing an

ancient boundary for which you will suffer consequences.

This verse goes on to emphasize the fact that "each one should know how to possess his own vessel in sanctification and honor, not in passion of lust, like those who do not know God". Are you acting like somebody who doesn't know God? You are not to have sex before marriage. You may be under the impression that this is the only Biblical sexual absolute. Not true! God is interested in more than just your technical virginity.

BOUNDARY #2: NO DATING UNBELIEVERS

"Do not be unequally yoked together with unbelievers. For what fellowship has righteousness with lawlessness? And what communion has light with darkness?"

—2 CORINTHIANS 6:14

Don't date an unbeliever. This is a sexual absolute. Don't send an e-mail accusing me of legalism. This is Bible. This is not up for debate.

"But Judah, she...she...I think she believes there's a God."

The Bible makes a clear distinction between believers and unbelievers. The term "Christian" was created to describe the early followers of the teachings of Jesus Christ. The word means "little Christ," which was appropriate because Jesus' disciples acted like Him, talked like Him, and had His characteristics. These days countless people walk around identifying themselves as Christians. Do they look like Jesus? Do they act like Jesus? Do they talk like Jesus? Do you? This is what it means to be a Christian. You are not to be in a romantic relationship with someone who is not a Christ follower.

"But Judah, he's coming to church with me now that we are dating. And if I break up with him now, he'll never get saved. So...I think God wants us to keep dating."

Wrong! God loves you too much to put you in a situation where you could potentially get your heart broken in order to see somebody saved. God specifically told us He would rather have us obey His Word than make sacrifices.

BOUNDARY #3: HOMOSEXUALITY IS SIN

"Because of this, God gave them over to shameful lusts. Even their women exchanged natural relations for unnatural ones. In the same way the men also abandoned natural relations with women and were inflamed with lust for one another. Men committed indecent acts with other men, and received in themselves the due penalty for their perversion." — **ROMANS 1:26-27**

Homosexuality is sin. Homosexuality is not natural. Christians tend to view homosexuality as the "unforgivable" sin and some may go so far as to justify having sex before marriage because they don't believe it to be quite as bad as committing a homosexual act. In truth, Jesus died on the cross to pay the penalty for all sin, including homosexuality.

It's amazing to me how our culture is handling the issue of homosexuality in young people. If you have one homosexual thought, your school counselor will say, "That's OK. That's just who you are." If you have one homosexual encounter your friends will tell you, "Well, I guess you're gay and we'll have to learn to accept you that way." If you have certain gifting or personality traits strangers will just expect you to be gay or a lesbian.

Don't give into the culture's way of thinking! Just because you've had homosexual thoughts or encounters, you are not destined to be gay. You sinned and you need to take that sin to the cross and allow Jesus to forgive you. God's amazing unconditional love for you didn't change with these acts. He has already paid the price on the cross. Homosexuality is sin — just like having sex before marriage and dating an unbeliever. You serve a God who is not intimidated by any type of sin and can empower you to overcome any challenge you are faced with.

BOUNDARY #4: NO SEXUAL TOUCHING

"Now concerning the things of which you wrote to me: It is good for a man not to touch a woman." —1 CORINTHIANS 7:1

The fourth absolute is no sexual touching. After reading **1 CORINTHIANS 7:1**, you men are probably thinking, "Excuse me? I can't even touch a woman?!" It's actually deeper than that. The word touch means "to cling sexually to; to touch sexually". This is an ancient boundary — a boundary that is just as relevant today as the day it was established.

"But I love her." There's no exception.

"But she said it was alright." No exception.

"But he said he'd marry me." No exception.

"What if we're touching over clothes?" Not okay.

No sexual touching. No petting. No playing around.

Have you ever been so hungry you eat a banana that isn't quite ripe? Deep inside you know it's not the right time to eat the banana but you tell yourself, "I'm sure it will be good." And it does taste good at first. Then you realize, as you experience that squeaky feeling on your teeth, the unripe banana was not ready to be eaten. Premature sexual touching will leave you with the same feeling. One of the hardest things I have to do is sit down with a couple who has "gone too far" and walk through the consequences with them.

If you see me interacting with young ladies in Generation Church, you will notice that I give side hugs. I do this to set an example and remain above reproach. You would be wise to conduct yourself in the same manner. No matter how you go about it, if your motivation for touching someone is impure you are overstepping an ancient boundary. This boundary has been put into place to preserve the sacredness of your sexuality. If we don't talk about these things your thinking will be influenced by cultural philosophies and your beliefs defined by extra-biblical ideologies.

↳ *Judah and his sister, Wendy*

BOUNDARY #5: TREAT ONE ANOTHER AS BROTHERS AND SISTERS

"Do not rebuke an older man, but exhort him as a father, younger men as brothers, older women as mothers, younger women as sisters, with all purity." —1 TIMOTHY 5:1-2

Now we're getting deeper. Young men, treat the young ladies like sisters. Young ladies, treat the young men like brothers. Most of you would never look at your brother the way you do the guys in your school. You men wouldn't entertain those thoughts about your sister. You think that's nasty? God agrees!

View and treat one another as brothers and sisters — minus the fighting, of course. This commandment changes everything. Some of you men will need to reevaluate the way you interact with ladies. You girls may have to think twice about what you are wearing before leaving the house. You wouldn't dream of walking by your brother's bedroom flaunting your body so why do you do it in the hallway at church? This leads us to boundary number six.

BOUNDARY #6: WEAR APPROPRIATE CLOTHING

"In like manner also, that the women adorn themselves in modest apparel, with propriety and moderation, not with braided hair or gold or pearls or costly clothing, but, which is proper for women professing godliness, with good works." —2 TIMOTHY 2:9-10

This portion of scripture instructs ladies to dress with dignity. The central issue here is not the brand of clothing you wear, the focus is whether or not you are dressing with the intention of drawing attention to your body. Are you covering your body, ladies? Gentlemen, do you need to pull up your pants?

The Bible challenges Christians in this area. This is a sexual absolute. Where it gets a bit shady is the definition of modesty, because modesty is interpreted differently in every culture. In India you can show your belly all day long but don't even think about showing your knees! So what is modest dressing for a teenage girl in the 21st Century going to high school in America?

Here is what my wife teaches girls about modesty. "It has to start on the inside. If the whole goal of your outfit is to draw attention to certain parts of your body, you're heading in the wrong direction. Ask yourself this question, 'What is the first thing somebody will notice when they look at me?' If your neckline is cut low, the first thing people will notice is your cleavage. If your skirt is so short you can't bend over, people will be distracted wondering how you're going to get that pencil you dropped. If your shirt is too short the poor guy next to you will be distracted during the entire worship service wondering what will happen when you lift up your hands to worship. The first thing people should notice about you is your countenance and the incredible joy you have. If you have to use your body to get attention, find new friends."

I will point out that the standards are different for a person who doesn't know God. There are frequently girls who visit our youth ministry wearing clothing that barely covers anything because they don't know any better. I'm speaking specifically to the ladies who are familiar with the standards and expectations. Don't walk around complaining that guys have no respect for you when you are showcasing everything God gave you. Dressing like a pop icon is not cool in church. You will actually end up feeling like less of a woman when you dress in a manner that attracts negative attention. You remove an ancient boundary when you put on that revealing shirt.

I know many young women who look trendy and beautiful while dressing appropriately and modestly. The Bible says that you should be recognized for your godliness and good works. People should be attracted to the God you serve.

BOUNDARY #7: NO LUSTFUL LOOKS

"You have heard that it was said to those of old, 'You shall not commit adultery.' "But I say to you that whoever looks at a woman to lust for her has already committed adultery with her in his heart."
—**MATTHEW 5:27-28 (NKJV)**

"I made a covenant with my eyes not to look lustfully at a girl."
—**JOB 31:1 (NIV)**

The Bible is very clear on this one: men are not to look lustfully at women and vice versa. Jesus explains that "anyone who looks at a woman lustfully has already committed adultery with her in his heart (**MATTHEW 5:27**)". The standard here is high for a reason. Why is the way you look at another person so important? Because "if the eye is clear and the eye is pure, the whole body will be full of light" **MATTHEW 22:22**. Are you filling your body with light or darkness? Looking at pornography is sin. Watching lewd movies is sin. **2TIMOTHY 2:22** in the New Living Translation instructs believers to "run from anything that stirs up youthful lust." There are no exceptions when it comes to what you view.

BOUNDARY #8: AVOID IMMORAL FRIENDS

"I wrote to you in my epistle not to keep company with sexually immoral people. Yet I certainly did not mean with the sexually immoral people of this world, or with the covetous, or extortioners, or idolaters, since then you would need to go out of the world. But now I have written to you not to keep company with anyone named a brother, who is sexually immoral, or covetous, or an idolater, or a reviler, or a drunkard, or an extortioner—not even to eat with such a person." —1 CORINTHIANS 5:9-11

This is the last boundary we will look at. Don't hang out with sexually immoral believers. This is very simple. You need to cut off friendships with people who call themselves Christians but continue to compromise their sexual standards.

Again, the Bible distinguishes between believers and non-believers in this instance. It is permissible to have non-Christian friends who don't live according to the standards you do. People who don't know God simply do not know better. You need to beware of people who profess to love God but don't live like Jesus.

BE TRANSFORMED

The only way you will be able to maintain these ancient boundaries is to be transformed by changing the way you think. You do this by recognizing, removing and replacing unclean thoughts. Romans 12:2 says, "do not be conformed to this world, but be transformed by the renewing of your mind." You are like the world when you think like the world. This is why changing external aspects of your life but continuing to adhere to worldly philosophies is nothing but beating the air. You must change your thought life. Failure to put a stop to ungodly thoughts and ideas leads to deception and an inability to discern the will of God. Romans explains that you must change the way you think in order to "prove what is that good and acceptable and perfect will of God." Your ability to control your thoughts directly influences your understanding of God's will for your life.

GIRD UP THE LOINS OF YOUR MIND

In **1 PETER 1:13**, Peter instructs Christians to "gird up the loins of [their] mind." This is a bizarre statement because, last time I checked, the loins and the mind are located in completely different parts of the body. When I was a boy my dad used to say, "Son, before you were born you were in my loins." My response was always, "Dad! I don't want to know about your loins! Don't tell me about your loins! That's weird!" Loins refer to the reproductive area of the body, but the Bible implies that there are loins in the mind. Your thoughts have loins? Yes! In fact, the thought you are thinking right now has loins. Every thought has reproductive power inherent within it. Some people are under the impression that they can live one way while thinking another. People actually believe that it is possible to carry on secret fantasies in their mind and still live like a man or woman of God. Be assured that your thoughts will catch up with you and be evidenced in the way you live your life.

The word "gird" was used in ancient Asian culture to describe an individual's gathering up of a long flowing robe. When embarking on a journey, a person would use leather straps to gird up their robe so that they would be unhindered in the trek. In the same way, when you begin a pursuit of purity you have to strap down impure thoughts and gird up imaginations in order to increase your aerodynamics and effectiveness. I am very leery of the random thoughts that run through the mind because they have destructive power within them. We all have moments when nasty thoughts

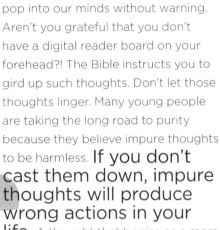

pop into our minds without warning. Aren't you grateful that you don't have a digital reader board on your forehead?! The Bible instructs you to gird up such thoughts. Don't let those thoughts linger. Many young people are taking the long road to purity because they believe impure thoughts to be harmless. **If you don't cast them down, impure thoughts will produce wrong actions in your life.** A thought that begins as a mere distraction will eventually steer you in the wrong direction. Wrong directions result in detours; detours lead to wrong destinations; and wrong destinations end in destruction.

If you don't change the way you think, these ancient boundaries will simply be a list of external rules and restrictions. COLOSSIANS 2:23 describes external efforts as rules that "may seem wise because they require strong devotion, pious self-denial, and severe bodily discipline" but "provide no help in conquering a person's evil desires."

If your purity has been reduced to a list of restrictions, you have limited something that is meant to be supernatural to your natural effort. The Bible teaches that rules seem wise because they require strong devotion but they are ineffective in producing internal change. You can research self-help strategies and apply seven steps to doing this or overcoming that but in the end you will still be wrestling the same fleshly desires.

So, how are you going to live pure? Choosing not to look at pornography is important but not the ultimate solution. **Your purity must start on the inside.**

My intention and prayer for you is that you will be internally and externally transformed as you consider these ancient boundaries and apply them to your life. These absolutes were set up for your security, satisfaction, fulfillment, and blessing, and they provide the foundation from which you can make wise decisions and discern the will of God. Even if you have lived up to this point outside of these guidelines, there is hope for your thinking and behavior to be transformed and aligned with Godly standards. God extends grace toward you for change.

Chapter 8
HAPPILY EVER AFTER

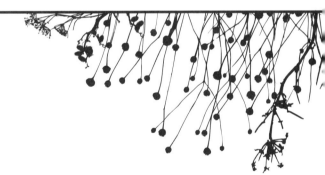

I want to conclude by talking with you about dating, relating, and relationships. This is a practical chapter that is pertinent to the stage of life many of you are in and I am excited to share biblically based relationship guidelines with you.

At this point you have begun to acknowledge the opposite sex; you have gone through puberty and have come to the realization that men and women are not the same. Eventually, you would like to get married. I have never met a young person who is looking forward to going through two or three marriages. I don't know any single people searching for a relationship that will leave them with a broken heart. Every person is desirous of a wholesome relationship; a romantic relationship that will provide satisfaction and fulfillment for a lifetime.

You may have noticed that healthy relationships don't happen by accident or occur coincidentally. The way you begin your romantic relationship can define its duration. In this chapter, I am going to share with you ten stages I have observed most happy and healthy couples go through as part of a dating and mating relationship progression.

According to **PROVERBS 18:22**, "he who finds a wife finds a good thing and obtains favor from the Lord." Before moving on we need to examine the original meaning of the words used in this verse because it would be easy to take this scripture at face value a reach a faulty conclusion. Lest you misinterpret Solomon's statement and venture out on a desperate quest for a spouse, let me point out that the word "find" literally

means "to come to at the end of a progression". You don't wake up one morning and decide to find a husband or wife. An appropriate process that couples must go through begins when two people become attracted to each other, relate respectfully to one another, set relationship standards, and eventually marry.

THE IMPORTANCE OF DATING RIGHT

Everyone wants a happy marriage. Unfortunately, I have observed couples who struggle to experience fulfillment in marriage because they didn't go about dating the right way. It is foolish to believe that you can date irresponsibly then enter into a healthy marriage. If you can't play well in the minor leagues you won't be able to function in the major leagues. Dating is an important issue because it has the potential to affect your marriage.

GOD CREATED FAMILY

God established the family unit. Family is sacred to God. I believe in the sanctity of marriage between one man and one woman. I believe that the marriage bed is holy. I believe that it is possible to experience total sexual fulfillment in the marriage bed. This is the way God intended it to be. I don't condone living with someone of the opposite sex before marriage with the purpose of discovering whether or not

you are sexually compatible. Such an arrangement is inconsistent with God's original plan.

God wants you to experience maximum fulfillment and, as your Creator, He knows exactly what will bring you joy. I recently read a magazine article about a newly-dating celebrity couple and realized that they wish they were living my life. They wish that they could experience love the way I do in my relationship with my wife. They are looking for what I have — maximum fulfillment and satisfaction. My wife is the only woman I have ever held hands with and the only woman I have slept with. When I spend time with Chelsea I am not thinking about previous relationships. We did not reach this level of intimacy by happenstance. We patterned our relationship after Biblical principles and had the sense to abide by the guidelines we established at the onset of our relationship. We are currently reaping the benefits of those decisions. You have a similar choice to make. One option would be to live without boundaries for the next several years and eventually reach the

conclusion that I was right all along. A better alternative would be choosing not to waste your time and put into practice the principles I am going to share with you. If you take these principles seriously you can be satisfied, fulfilled, and blessed — I guarantee it!

WHERE TO GO FROM HERE: RELATIONSHIP STAGES

Most of you would agree that marriage is a sacred institution. You probably even understand that the dating relationship significantly impacts the success of a marriage. Questions arise when it comes to initiating a relationship. Many are confused concerning the way to go about getting to know the person they are interested in. A big issue in churches is whether we are "daters" or "courters." Are we relaters, maters, friends, not friends, more than friends, romantic, not romantic? If we don't respond to these questions with biblically based answers, relationships within the church will end up mirroring those in Hollywood. Media has taught us that, when you

like someone, you kiss first, have sex, then decide where the relationship is going. As Christians, we know that this progression is not right! We believe that sex is more than a biological act that meets a biological desire. We believe in marriage and the sanctity of sex. We advocate respecting a person for who they are, not just admiring the way their skin is stretched over their skeletal frame.

So if you are not taking cues from Hollywood, where do you start when it comes to dating and mating? The Bible does not provide specific steps for dating relationships because it was designed to transcend time and culture. The ten relationship stages I am going to introduce to you are my interpretation of the way couples should go about dating in current culture using Biblical principles as the standard. I don't believe these stages to be absolutes but I am confident that if you implement them you will be rewarded and live without regret.

THE FAITH PERIOD

As discussed in the previous chapter, the Bible teaches that believers and non-believers are not to be unequally yoked. When you become attracted to someone you need to spend time evaluating the substance of their faith. Does this person have a genuine faith in Jesus Christ that is evidenced in the way they live? Before you plan an elaborate marriage proposal, it is critical that you assess what kind of relationship they have with Jesus. If your response is, "I'm pretty sure she's a Christian. She wears a gold necklace with a cross on it. She even goes to Handel's Messiah every year at Christmas time. She must be a Christian," you better step back. If it isn't obvious from a distance that a person is a follower of Christ, it is likely that they aren't. Go no further if that turns out to be the case!

I have had the advantage of knowing my wife Chelsea since we were in the church nursery. We grew up attending church together until my family moved away when I was 13 years old. Even after that point I saw her periodically.

↳ *Judah & Chelsea (spotlighted) at ages 4 and 5*

↳ *Judah & Chelsea in Junior High.*

I specifically remember preaching at a Junior High Camp in Portland, Oregon where Chelsea was working as an administrative assistant. I wasn't interested in her romantically at the time but recall thinking, "Wow! Chelsea has a great relationship with God." I even prayed over her at one of the services, declaring that she was a woman of God who would one day have a ministry of her own and didn't need a husband to complete her. How ironic!

You will get yourself into trouble if you skip this first step. If you attempt to develop a romantic relationship with someone who has no faith in God you will end up on the wrong track. If you overlook stage one but conduct yourself appropriately throughout the remainder of your time together, God will be unable to honor the relationship. I don't believe in "flirt to convert." I'm not in favor of "missionary marriage." Such strategies are not Biblical.

THE FRIENDSHIP PERIOD

One of my favorite relationship stages is the friendship period. A friendship must be established before attraction is communicated. The foundation for a strong marriage is a great friendship. My wife and I go out on a date once a week and I am often disappointed to observe other couples sitting in restaurants with nothing to say to each other. Believe it or not, the majority of your married life will not be spent having sex! Marriage is about living life with another person on a daily basis. If you fail to establish a friendship early on it will be impossible for you to go through life together. Your relationship must be built on more than physical attraction if you intend to progress any further.

I will never forget the weekend in December of 1998 when Chelsea and her family came from Portland, Oregon to

Seattle, Washington to visit my family for the holidays. Spending time together during the Christmas season had been a tradition for years but something was different this time. On this particular weekend Chelsea and I talked more than we ever had in the past. It was so much fun! We spent most of the visit hanging out with our families as we got to know each other better. One of the best ways to establish a friendship is in a group setting. Spending time with another person exclusively can raise premature expectations and relationship definitions can become unclear. The safest and easiest way to create a friendship is to hang out in groups. Now I sound like your mom or dad or your distant uncle who is a pastor, don't I?

THE FAMILY PERIOD

This stage of a relationship can be easily overlooked, particularly if you are over eighteen (which you probably should be when you begin the process of dating).

I have yet to come across a scripture that reads, "Thus saith the Lord, 'Now that you are eighteen years old you are free to make all your own decisions."

Regardless of your age or season of life, you must involve parents and family in your relationship by way of inviting their input and seeking their approval. I don't care if it takes until you are forty-six to find your soul mate! Call up your eighty year old dad and include him in the process. There has to be a family stage!

↳ *Judah & Chelsea with their families and pastors.*

Why is involving your family so important? Family members know you better than anyone else. Even non-Christian family members want the best for you and need to be included. This stage comes before the next, which is "feelings", because the moment feelings are communicated commitment begins to form. It is appropriate to receive the support of your family before you spill your feelings. This process should also include members of your spiritual family, such as pastors and small group leaders.

I knew I was on the right track when I shared my feelings for Chelsea with my mom, dad, sister, and youth pastor, and all were supportive of my plans to pursue her. Meanwhile, Chelsea was talking with her family and leaders about me. I wish I would have known that at the time because it would have made the next step a lot easier for me.

THE FEELINGS PERIOD

Gentlemen, you've got to have the guts to communicate your intentions. Ladies, if you are attracted to a guy who appears to share your interest but doesn't have the courage to communicate his feelings toward you, drop him like a bad habit. Men need to have enough sense and discernment to recognize and acknowledge that spending time together creates some level of emotional commitment. Such a realization should motivate a man to bring definition to the relationship. Guys, you are not ready for a relationship if you are content to continue flirting without sharing feelings. Feelings and intentions need to be communicated in the proper timing.

I would like to say that I handled this step like a real pro, but that wasn't exactly the case. Chelsea and I were talking on the phone on Christmas day when I finally got up the courage to tell her that I was going to ask for her dad's permission to pursue a relationship with her. "So does that mean you like me?" was Chelsea's response. I suppose I could have been more eloquent in the way I communicated my feelings, but the important thing was that I shared them.

THE FOUNDATION PERIOD

Once you begin sharing feelings a foundation needs to be laid. When feelings come into play hands want to touch things; lips want to kiss. If you don't lay a foundation for

dating your emotions will rule your relationship. What do I mean by foundation? I'm referring to standards you are going to abide by while dating. Your foundation must line up with God's Word and should be based on the boundaries discussed in the last chapter. The purpose of the foundation is to keep you within those boundaries. Make your boundaries clear. I recommend making yourself accountable to your family and leaders. Gentlemen, it is primarily your responsibility to initiate the foundation stage.

You ever been camping or hiking? When people go hiking without a map or a compass they often tie markers on trees so that, no matter how deep into the woods they venture, they can find their way out of the forest. The stages I am introducing to you are relationship markers. No matter how involved you get with another person, you can always turn around and find your way out of the forest of romance and relationship. Let's say that the two of you start sharing feelings but your intentions don't match up. You have

the option to admit incompatibility and agree not to go any farther. If that happens you can still remain friends; you can honor one another even if you attend the same church and end up marrying different people. You've got to establish the foundation. You have to leave markers on trees. So far I have given you five markers.

I am proud to report that I honored the progression, established appropriate boundaries, and respected Chelsea while we dated. If Chelsea and I had broken up the night before our wedding we would have made it safely out of the forest. Sure, things would have been uncomfortable for a time, but I would have been able to look her in the eyes and know I had valued her as my girlfriend.

THE FUN PERIOD

Relationships should be fun! You should enjoy getting to know one another, going on dates, and talking. Setting clear standards allows you to have fun when spending time together. In

Generation Church we have a saying: "fun isn't fun unless it's still fun in the morning." Tomorrow will you be proud of the decisions you made today? Will you regret that you touched her there or stayed out too late? You want to look back on your dating season as a time that was fun!

My wife loves to go hiking so I planned a hike for her twenty-first birthday. I looked up directions to the trailhead, packed a map, laced up my hiking boots, and we set off. We enjoyed the car ride together and were so excited about the adventure but never ended up finding the trail! What a birthday! Chelsea and I had fun while dating, even when our plans didn't work out.

THE FUTURE PERIOD

After you've shared feelings, laid a foundation, and are having fun together, it's time to consider where the relationship is headed. Gentlemen, you need to initiate a conversation about the future of your relationship. The timing of this stage is different for every couple but there comes a point when you need to talk about the direction the relationship is going. I'm not implying that you have to bring up the subject of marriage, but it is critical that you determine what the future looks like.

You need to spend time in prayer and may even want to fast. Allow God to speak to you about the relationship. If you aren't given clear direction from God it would be wise to spend a season apart from one another. It is better to be safe than sorry. If there is no future in the relationship this is the time to follow the markers out of the woods.

THE FINANCIAL PERIOD

After you've talked about the future ladies, you need to consider the state of his finances. I know he may be hot. I know that when he holds you in his arms all your troubles seem to melt away, but ask yourself, "Does he have a job?" Don't marry someone who doesn't have the ability to maintain employment. Guys, has the woman you are considering marrying put her life on hold in search of a man who can bring her definition and direction? I didn't marry that kind of woman. I knew that Chelsea was going to change the world whether I married her or not and I wanted to join her team. You have to understand that you individually have a purpose outside of a relationship with another person. God has a plan just for you! This is practical. When you enter into marriage you become financially responsible to and for another person. Does he or she have a job? Is he or she in thousands of dollars of consumer debt? This element cannot be overlooked.

THE FIANCÉ PERIOD

This is the stage where the big question is asked. "Will you marry me?" This is a season of celebration. It is also the period where you must seriously consider for the last time the commitment you have made to one another. Do you really want to follow through with marrying this person? Even if you reach this point but feel you are making a wrong decision you can back out with honor. Unfortunately, people in church circles seem to believe that once a couple starts dating they eventually have to get married. This is not the case. You need to walk in obedience to God's will and evaluate whether or not this particular relationship is right for you.

THE FAVOR PERIOD

This is what you've been waiting for — a time to enjoy the favor of God! "Surely there is a reward for the righteous" PSALM 58:11. As a pastor, it is a privilege to be involved in marriages and observe God's favor on relationships. I've presided over many weddings and nothing compares with watching a happy couple celebrate the beginning of a marriage relationship surrounded by people who love them. Such times of celebration are a result of the favor of God. I believe that it is God's plan for you to have a beautiful relationship and fulfilling marriage that lasts a lifetime. God intends for you to live happily ever after. I remind you though, that good mating starts with good dating.

REWARDS FOR DOING THINGS RIGHT

Chelsea and I experience God's favor in our marriage and our lives. Favor shows up in the form of great friendship, good communication, provision, and total fulfillment. It is my prayer for you that years down the road you and your spouse will sit across the table from one another and still have something to laugh about. I want you to experience the confidence and satisfaction that comes from knowing you married your best friend. By this point you should recognize that God honors and rewards holiness and obedience. If you allow God to remain at the center of your relationships and conduct yourself according to Biblical standards, you can expect that "goodness and mercy will follow [you] all the days of [your] life" (PSALM 23:6).

I believe you can live pure.

ENDNOTES

ENDNOTES

Chapter 1 The Beautiful Affliction

1 Thom S. Rainer, The Bridger Generation: America's Second Largest Generation, What They Believe, How to Reach Them (Nashville, TN: Broadman & Holman Publishers, 1997).

Chapter 4 Crouching, Craving, Chasing

2 Alanna Nash, Reader's Digest, April 2004.

NOTES

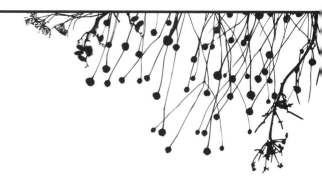

JUDAHS

OTHER DATING DELILAH RESOURCES

WORKBOOK

AUDIOBOOK ON CD

AUDIOBOOK ON MP3

COLOPHON

Produced on **Apple Computers** using **Adobe Creative Suite 3**

Title, header and body text is set in **Gotham**

Scripture, quotations and reference text is set in **Archer**

Both typefaces designed by Hoefler & Frere-Jones (typography.com)

High-resolution brushes courtesy Jason Gaylor (designfruit.com)

Additional imagery gathered from various stock sources

Special thanks to **DeMonnin's Art Studio, Inc.**